The Green Season

Other Books by Robert Isenberg

The Archipelago: A Balkan Passage

Wander

The Iron Mountain

In Defense of the Turtleneck

How to Ride a Bike in Pittsburgh

The Legend of Pangkor

The Pittsburgh Monologue Project
(with Brad Keller)

The Green Season

Robert Isenberg

THE TICO TIMES
PUBLICATIONS GROUP

Copyright © 2015 by Robert Isenberg

All rights reserved. Except for brief excerpts in published reviews, no part of this book may be reproduced, stored in a retrieval system, or transmitted in any form or by any means, electronic, mechanical, photocopying, recording, or otherwise, without written permission from the publisher. To contact the publisher from within Costa Rica, write to The Tico Times, Publications Group, Avenida 11 entre calles 5 y 7, edificio blanco con rotulo The Tico Times, Carmen, San José, San José, 10101. To contact the publisher from outside Costa Rica, write to The Tico Times, Publications Group, P.O. Box 025331, SJO 717, Miami, FL 33102-5331, USA. For further contact information, visit www.ticotimes.net.

Excerpts from this book first appeared in *The Tico Times, The Smart Set, Hippocampus,* and *Medium.*

ISBN-13: 978-9968-47-877-9 (paper)

The Tico Times Publications Group
Avenida 11 entre calles 5 y 7
San José, Costa Rica

First published 2015
Published simultaneously in Costa Rica and the United States of America

Cover art by Haime Luna
Book design by Gabriela Wattson

10 9 8 7 6 5 4 3 2 1

For Kylan
Pura vida, mi amor.

Contents

Author's Note ix
Prologue xi

El Barrio

Our Apartment: A Field Guide 3
Who Watches the *Guachimán*? 17
The Autobús Diaries 21

La Gente

Beach Town 31
The Last War Hero 39
City by the Sea 49
Day of the Devils 59
The Working Poet 67
Saving Hearts 77

Unas Aventuras

Wiping Out 91
Oral History 97
Pirates of the Caribbean 105
Moving Pictures 111
Inside the Refugio 117
Bioluminescent in Bocas 123

La Temporada Verde

How to Survive the Rainy Season 131
Car Trouble 137

Acknowledgments 145

Author's Note

Most of the essays in this book first appeared in *The Tico Times*, although some were included in other hospitable publications. I have changed, rewritten, and embellished every piece to make it more readable in book form. They are all works of nonfiction, but in some cases names have been changed. Events are presented as truthfully as I am capable of recounting them.

For many reasons, this is my favorite kind of book to read—a collection of shorter writings, printed and distributed over the course of months or years. According to legend, editor Phil Graham once called journalism "the first draft of history," but that history is often the author's as much as the world's. Such collections behave like diaries, documenting what the journalist saw and heard over a period of time. Readers are transported to exotic places and meet interesting people, but they do so through the perspective of the writer, whose temperament changes daily. Each subject demands a distinct style, approach, and word-count. Every chapter is different, and the reader can skip around with impunity.

Indeed, I hope that people read The Green Season the same way they would eat a casado. As everyone in Costa Rica knows, casado means "married" but refers to an ubiquitous lunch platter: There's rice, beans, salad, plantains, and some kind of meat. A freshly blended fruit drink is usually included, plus maybe a cup of coffee and a tiny bowl of sherbet. This has become my favorite noontime meal, not just in Costa Rica, but anywhere. Some things taste better than others, but as an ensemble the *casado* is more than the sum of its flavors.

Prologue

HERE'S WHAT HAPPENS.

I hail a taxi in the rain, rip open the door, and dive into the back seat, folding my umbrella as I go. I'm careful not to slam the door, because *taxistas* hate that.

"San Rafael de Escazú," I bellow in breathless Spanish. "There's a restaurant called La Cascada. My apartment is near there."

"*Claro, con gusto,*" says the driver, and we bomb down the street, narrowly missing some skinny kids in hoodies as they trot across the rain-spattered pavement. For some reason I don't have to give any more directions, because all the *taxistas* in San José know about La Cascada, the famous steakhouse that every single Costa Rican describes as *very good, and very expensive.*

"How's your night going?" I ask.

"Slow," says the cabbie. Then he adds, as an afterthought, "*Pura vida.*"

A few blocks later, as we skirt the tiered plaza of the National Museum, the cabbie asks, "Where are you from?"

"The United States. Pennsylvania." Not exactly true, but I spent enough time in Pittsburgh to claim I'm "from" there, and few Ticos have ever heard of Vermont.

"How do you like Costa Rica?"

"I love it."

"How long are you visiting?"

"I live here, actually."

"*¿Al chile?*" he exclaims. *For real?*

There's a pause. The radio plays some Christian rock song in Spanish, and drizzle spritzes through the cracked window, and the windshield is so fogged up that I can barely see the battered sidewalks and gated cement buildings scrolling past at inadvisable speeds. I'm very tipsy, but not drunk, because Costa Rican beers are laughably weak. I'm feeling *muy tranquilo*, despite the rapidly ticking meter.

Without fail, by the time we reach the backstreets of Paseo Colón, where the neighborhood is lifeless and traffic lights mean nothing, the cabbie asks: "How did you come to Costa Rica?"

Good question.

What do I tell this *taxista*? This conversation happens again and again, and every driver is slightly different. Maybe he is an old man, a fat man, a skinny soccer fanatic, a Panamanian with a mustache and mullet who swears every other word. Maybe he ashes a cigarette out the window, or he touches a dangling rosary at every intersection. Whoever he is—and it is always an *hombre*, never a *mujer*—I get this question, and I have to think, *How did I get here? Where do I start?*

Every Gringo has a story, and *que mae*, most of our stories are long and convoluted. Maybe we fell in love with some beach town. Maybe we came for a month of soul-searching and never left. A girlfriend brought us, or a real estate deal. We work for an online gambling outfit, or we started a yoga studio. We came here as students, some years ago, but we returned to *really live*, this time. Maybe we married a Tico. Or we love to surf, dude. Or we're running from the law. Or—it's upsettingly common—we just showed up, flipped through a Spanish phrasebook, and blew all our money on booze, complaining to anyone who would listen about how hard it is to find a job.

You hear a lot of those stories. But none of those people are me.

¿Entonces, por qué?

How do I explain a random visit to a Mexican restaurant with my girlfriend Kylan? This place called Gran Agave, back in Pittsburgh, where we lived for so many years. We went inside, where the air was cool and a smiling host offered us a wooden booth. We sat by the window, perused the menus, and talked excitedly over glasses of Coca-Cola. When we ordered, the waiter smiled warmly, bowed his head, touched his heart, and disappeared to the kitchen.

"I just love Latin culture," Kylan said. "It's so warm and hospitable."

"I didn't realize you liked it so much," I admitted. I knew that Kylan had spent some time in Cuba, where her Quaker private school performed volunteer work. I also knew that she had once spoken conversational Spanish. But I had never appreciated her passion for Latin America. She looked dreamy now, gazing at the pastel-colored décor of Gran Agave. Even our free basket of tortilla chips and salsa tasted like sunshine.

"Would you ever live down there?"

"Sure," she said.

"I've always wanted to live abroad," I said.

"Where would you want to live?"

"Costa Rica."

"Really? Why?"

I recited my list of long-rehearsed reasons: tropical weather, stable government, expansive national parks, no military, famously happy people—and that golden reputation, gushed about by every hippie and backpacker I'd met since the late 1990s. Costa Rica was a special place, they said, a mecca for forward thinking, pure living, carefree times, communing with nature, drinking organic coffee with people who really appreciated life.

"Have you ever been there?" Kylan asked. She knew I'd traveled a lot, but my past itineraries were hard to keep straight, even for someone I'd dated for five years.

"No."

"We should go," she said.

"Yeah, we should."

That conversation seems long ago, on this drizzly night in San José. The *taxista* pauses at the highway, and then we careen left, past La Sabana Park, where glistening trees envelop the lawns in darkness.

I think of our first trip to San José. Arriving in Costa Rica was a blur of passport control and yowling cabbies. We had no idea what to expect. We took a bus downtown, and we spent nearly two hours trying to find our hotel. There were no street signs or numbers. The tangled lanes were filled with trash and barbed wire. We asked people on the sidewalk where to go, but they only looked both ways down the street, as if they had lost their bearings, too.

When we finally found the hotel, the room was small and the beds were full of little black bugs. When night fell—at 5 p.m.—the grim streets terrified us, and we decided to drink cans of beer in the safety of our room.

When we emerged the next morning, we took a walk through an urban park. The teenagers were rowdy and pretended to fistfight each other. A ruddy man approached. He wore a dirty T-shirt and his black hair was combed over greasily.

"English?" he said.

"Uh, yes?"

He showed us a fist full of highlighters.

"I am selling these to people to make money," the man said. He swayed slightly, as if dizzy or distracted. "I am HIV-positive, and I want to eat something, and this is the way I make money on the street…"

We gave him some coins and walked hurriedly away.

Costa Rica was *not* love at first sight.

But then we took a bus to the town of La Fortuna. The inner city melted away, and the foothills emerged, rolling playfully beneath billowy clouds.

As the suburbs faded into fields and forest, and the bus climbed into rolling countryside, Costa Rica emerged as an actual country. The open windows admitted streams of fresh air. The seats vibrated beneath us, as if echoing our anxious excitement. The complex landscape scrolled past the dust-matted windows—blankets of greenery accentuated by the rainy season. Clusters of houses were like plaster dots connected by a narrow line of road.

In La Fortuna, we did what tourists were supposed to do in Costa Rica: We zip-lined in the rainforest. We hiked into a ravine, where we discovered a waterfall and splashed in its rippling pool, even as a thunderstorm swirled above and droplets dribbled through the foliage. We rode a motorboat across Lake Arenal and arrived in the cloud forests of Santa Elena, where strips of fog elegantly draped the mountains, and multicolored hammocks called to us. We joined a night hike in the jungle, where our guide shone his flashlight on tree frogs and poisonous snakes and cyanide-filled millipedes.

This was how Costa Rica won us over. We stopped into a *soda* for lunch and ate our first *casado*—that perfect mix of rice, beans, salad, and filet of fish—and we pictured ourselves eating this meal every day, drinking a cup of fresh mango juice whenever we wanted. The image stuck with us. We flew away with a mission in mind: We would live in Costa Rica, one way or another.

When we returned to the United States, we started to hatch our plot. We spent a full year preparing, and then we unloaded everything we owned. We sold our house. We sold Kylan's car. We sold our iMac and wraparound couch. We even sold our clothes and silverware, and whatever we couldn't sell, we gave away. Friends inherited paintings and textbooks and global knickknacks.

Then we celebrated: For a solid month, Pittsburghers threw us farewell parties. We drank and hugged and promised to Skype each other. We vowed to visit as soon as we could. We promised a spot on our future sofa to whomever cared to visit us in Central America. Finally we drove away from our beloved Steel City, and that was that.

"How long have you worked as a taxi driver?" I ask.

"Fifteen years," says the driver quickly, because every *taxista* knows exactly how long he's been driving.

"How do you like it?"

"I like it," he says, but he's tentative. "I meet people from around the world. Many interesting people. But sometimes it's dangerous, especially at night." Then I hear a story about a passenger in Desamparados who threatened him with a machete. Or a thug threw a rock at his windshield, or some woman who refused to pay for a long ride. There's always a grim tale, and after reliving past trauma, he's eager to change the subject.

"What do you do for work?" the *taxista* asks.

"I'm a journalist," I say. "I write for the English-language newspaper."

"*¡Qué bonito!*" the *taxista* says. He has heard of *The Tico Times*, because many Costa Ricans used to read the newspaper religiously, back when it was published on actual paper. Ever since the paper became an online publication, fewer Ticos realize it still exists. But they have fond memories of the old days, when the paper was still stacked at newsstands. The driver seems relieved to know that it perseveres in digital form. "What do you write about?"

"Arts, culture, travel," I say. "Interesting people. Stuff like that."

Now the driver reevaluates me, because I seem to be a different kind of Gringo—someone who lives here, speaks conversational Spanish, and works for a local company. I am not a pushy backpacker trying to score pot. I'm not the retiree who shouts an address and sits back in silence. Indeed, the *taxista* seems pleased to have a writer in his cab.

"My name is Miguel," he says, and he extends a hand behind his back, so I can shake it.

"Robert," I say.

"*Mucho gusto.*"

And now we are no longer strangers.

As if on cue, Miguel says, "You speak Spanish very well."

"Thank you," I say, knowing that "well" is a relative term, but I'm always delighted to bumble through a conversation in my fifth half-learned language, making decent small talk in the safety of a taxicab. This guy has no idea what an uphill battle Spanish has been for me, but *poco a poco* is the rule in Costa Rica. People forgive my bad conjugations, my odd word choice, my complete misuse of the subjunctive. Sometimes I hold great conversations, talking for hours about all kinds of things. Other times, I just blink and grimace, because I have no idea what people are saying to me.

"Do you speak any English?" I ask.

"A *leetle beet*," Miguel says in English, pinching his fingers.

And we both laugh.

As the cab climbs the highway, and we take an exit that curves toward Escazú, Miguel asks: "What do you like about Costa Rica?"

Where to begin? I could tell him how much I love the hills and valleys, the dense rainforest and sprawling beaches, the toucans and ceviche by the sea. I could wax poetic about the beauty of Tica girls, the taste of *agua de pipa* after a roadside vendor cracks open a coconut shell with her machete.

But the truth is, those are the passing affections of a tourist. You can relish a Pacific sunset over Tamarindo on your first day in Costa Rica and rappel down a canyon the next morning. That's the stuff that won us over. But Kylan and I live here now, and it takes a lot of work to love Costa Rica on its own terms. The "authentic culture" that everyone seeks requires some digging, and I don't mean a two-hour visit to the Jade Museum. Ticos are polite and accommodating, but they are a private people. Breaking the ice with a new Costa Rican friend always feels like a victory. The country is subtle and hard to figure out. Everybody says *pura vida*, but I could spend a lifetime figuring out what it really means.

In that moment, I remember that the Tourism Ministry doesn't call this time of year "the rainy season," but rather "the green season." It's their upbeat way of looking at the torrential downpours.

I like this perspective. It's much like my life here. Costa Rica can be hard—soggy, bureaucratic, bad roads, long nights—but the challenges are invigorating. I've heard it many times, many ways: When the rain falls hardest, the country is most alive.

What I love about Costa Rica—and disdain, and gawk at, and find hilarious—can't be summarized in a few sentences. So I just say, "*Muchas cosas*," and then I point outside and add, "*Aquí, por fa'*." Miguel pulls to the curb of my darkened street. When I hand Miguel a little too much cash and insist, "*No cambio*," he thanks me and drives off, never realizing how badly I have wanted to know his land and people, how thoroughly it has already affected me. To even scratch the surface, I would need an entire book of impressions and anecdotes, essays and articles, conversations and mistakes and triumphs.

Miguel may never read that book. But for you, here it is.

El Barrio

Our Apartment: A Field Guide

Species *Felis catus*

We brought our cats to Costa Rica. None of our friends could believe it. "You're bringing your cats?" they asked.

But we couldn't leave them behind. Oscar and Felix are like our children. Oh, we could sell the car, donate our wardrobes, switch off our iPhones indefinitely, but we couldn't abandon our cats. So we made the special visit to the veterinarian in Doylestown. We asked for the special paperwork. We ordered the special cat-carriers that the airline had approved. We paid the extra fares when we bought our tickets. We stuffed Oscar and Felix into their little compartments and Kylan's mother drove us to the airport. The cats mewled for a while as we merged onto the highway, then gradually they got quiet.

At the security checkpoint, I had to remove Felix from the carrier and present her to a TSA officer. I carried her in my arms through the metal detector, and then another TSA officer had to pat her down—presumably to check for the bomb she might be stashing in her fur. Felix is skittish anyway, and the busy airport, with its shouting security guards and constant motion, made her shiver with terror. Felix dug her claws into my shirt and buried her face in my shoulder. But then it was over: I zipped her back into the carrier, and we boarded the plane. We stuck both carriers under our seats, as instructed, and both cats were silent the entire flight to San José.

"I can't believe how good they're being," Kylan whispered to me, somewhere over the dark Caribbean.

"It's insane," I concurred.

"Soon they'll be *jungle cats*," said Kylan.

This had been our longstanding joke—Oscar and Felix would become "jungle cats." They would run freely in the Central American wilderness, befriending animals and lazing in the tropical sun. "They're going to chase geckos!" we exclaimed. We pictured them playing benevolently with lizards in our adobe villa. This was a fantasy, of course. Our cats had rarely left the house, much less wandered around outside. But it painted a pleasant picture of our new life.

When we arrived at Juan Santamaría Airport, long after dark, we passed through Immigration without so much as a raised eyebrow. Kylan insisted on showing a security guard our special paperwork, but he only nodded at it, confused. The guard then leaned into Oscar's carrier, smiled broadly, and said, "¡Hola, gatito!"

Family Formicidae

Our first apartment was small and strange, and we knew we couldn't stay there long. Kylan's colleague, a retired expatriate named Harry, had offered to rent the studio to us, and we were grateful for somewhere to land. The rent was cheap and the place was pre-furnished. I could theoretically hop on a bus and arrive at my office in about 45 minutes. Perfect.

But the moment we arrived, late at night, we started to draft an exit plan. The wooden floors were so ragged that we could see light between the floorboards. The kitchen appliances were miniature, like Fischer-Price toys, and the mini-fridge was mounted atop a rickety wood platform. The kitchen table was small and stuck in the corner, and the front balcony was only large enough to store bags of trash. The mattress was so rigid that I considered sleeping on the floor. The second bedroom was basically empty, except for a freestanding coat hanger, so we stuck the cats' litter box in the corner.

We couldn't complain, though. Harry had spared us expensive weeks in a hotel, and he had asked for nothing in return. The average Tico earns $10,000 per year, and such living conditions are typical. The apartment was perfectly functional for the short term.

Then one morning, as I boiled water in a frying pan to make instant coffee, Kylan yelped.

"What's wrong?" I said.

"*Ants!*" she cried, pointing to the table.

The ants were microscopic. They were barely visible, much less harmful. But there were hundreds of them, marching in a fluid caravan. The queue of ants poured out of a crease in the wallpaper, corkscrewed across the wall, crossed the floor, flowed up a steel table leg, and finally pooled in a coffee mug—the same mug I had intended to use.

From then on, Kylan stuck any open bag or box in the refrigerator. Kylan has always been a fastidious cleaner, but the ants made her even more compulsive: She wiped down every surface multiple times a day. She sprayed and scrubbed and mopped. Normally her cleanliness struck me as obsessive, but I couldn't argue with the evidence: A single drip of marinara sauce on the counter could attract legions of bugs. The ants drizzled out of the windowsill and teemed atop the tiniest crumb.

"Did you eat a piece of bread last night?" Kylan demanded. Or: "Did you wash that spoon yet?"

I am a sloppy and thoughtless eater, and Kylan's hatred for the ants caused constant stress. When we finally bought a saucepot, I had to stir slowly, lest a single granule of rice or droplet of soup fall between the stove and the sink, arousing biblical pestilence.

After only five days, we started scouring Craigslist for a new place to live.

Order Araneae

The real estate agent's name was Adriana, and the moment we met her on a back street in Escazú, we knew we liked her.

"This apartment just went on the market," she said in perfect English. "You're the first people to see it."

She unlocked the iron gate and guided us across a short driveway and through the front door. When it swung open and we saw the spacious kitchen inside, I exclaimed, "Can we just tell you *yes, we'll take it?*"

Adriana chuckled uncomfortably. She was a sweet young woman who had recently studied in Colorado, but she still didn't know how to handle my raging Gringo enthusiasm. "Why don't we see the rest of the apartment first?" she suggested.

"Right, yes, of course!" I said breathlessly, and we followed her into the living room.

The apartment was beautiful, with its wooden sideboard, slatted closet doors, high ceilings, and three modest skylights. The furniture was tastefully chosen and actually matched. The cream-colored walls begged for artful décor. It was more than we could have hoped for, especially in the first month of our Costa Rican life.

"And here is the back patio," said Adriana as she unlocked a glass door and ushered us outside.

The space was small but splendid. A plastic table sat beneath a glass roof, and an uncovered section of the patio was ringed with exotic plants. It was perfect for lounging, hanging laundry, setting out cat litter—

"I *am* curious about the spiders," I said.

"Spiders?" said Adriana. She turned around and paused. "Huh, I guess I hadn't noticed those before."

What Adriana hadn't noticed were a dozen arachnids hanging motionless in the air. Their webs crisscrossed the patio, and each creature was suspended at eye-level. Their black bodies were the size of dimes and speckled with color, and their legs splayed several inches in every direction. They looked mechanical and streamlined; their legs were as thick and sturdy as hairpins. They were the largest and most fearsome-looking spiders I had ever seen in real life.

Still, we took the apartment. We moved all our belongings the very next day. We were elated, of course, to live on a quiet street full of comfortable modern houses. We appreciated the guard post at the front of the *urbanización*, the pre-installed WiFi and cable TV, the hot-water shower and generous spare room. These are luxuries many Ticos do not enjoy. But we were wary of the back patio. We didn't even discuss it. For weeks, we avoided that space as we silently debated what to do about the spiders.

Finally we caved.

"You want to just spray them?" Kylan suggested.

"I'm okay with that if you are," I said.

I have been severely arachnophobic my entire life. The thought of cohabitating with spiders gave me constant nightmares. If we bought one can of Raid and sprayed them discreetly, surely that would solve all our problems. And what if they were venomous? Weren't we just protecting ourselves from danger?

We sprayed one afternoon, and one by one the spiders struggled and writhed. Each spider descended a long silken string until it reached the ground, its long legs clawing at the air until it finally stopped moving. The murders were sad and horrible, and I acknowledged that the spiders had done nothing wrong. If anything, they ate other insects. But when the spiders had finally expired, and we wrecked their webs with a broom, we felt better. They could live anywhere they liked, we decided. Just not in our patio.

Class Aves

We rarely saw birds, but we could hear them: Unlike the songbirds we knew from Pennsylvania summers, these birds squawked and chattered all morning long. We woke to hear them in neighbors' trees. They hopped over our skylights and pecked at the metal roof. Sometimes I thought I heard a bird hit our roof, but later we realized it was the sound of a mango falling off an overhanging branch, which I suppose explained the rolling sound.

Order Blattodea

Kylan screamed and jumped away from the bathroom. I spotted the cockroach and cried out in alarm. The thing was enormous, larger than any cockroach I had ever seen. It scampered across the tile, trying to reach the sideboard and disappear behind its shelves. I grabbed a shoe and slammed it down. The cockroach's body exploded, shooting pale guts in all directions. The exoskeleton was shattered, but its legs continued to wiggle in a frantic attempt to live.

The roaches came in all sizes. They dwelt in our cabinets and skulked among our toiletries. They appeared at random times, traveling the floors like commuters off to work. We chased them, crushed them, and dumped them in the street. Most were big; some were enormous. I hadn't seen a cockroach in years, not since my dorm room days, and now they were everywhere.

"I'm sorry," said Kylan. "We *have* to get an exterminator. I can't live like this."

But after our Raid experiment, we couldn't stomach more chemicals, so Kylan tracked down a "green" pest-control service.

The exterminator arrived on a moped. He was a convivial middle-aged man, and he carried all his gear with him, precariously balanced on his two-wheeled vehicle. He sprayed down the apartment with a concoction made of cottonseed oil. The whole process took only a matter of minutes. He gave Kylan an unexpected discount, smiled warmly, hopped on his moped, and rode away.

For the next few hours, a dozen roaches emerged from their hiding places to die operatically on the kitchen floor. Their bodies seemed to break open, and their innards dissolved into slimy pools. Kylan was horrified, but she also relished watching them expire.

"I had no idea there were so many of them," Kylan told me when I got home from work. "And it's guaranteed for six months!"

Order Isoptera

We never saw the termites, and to this day I'm not sure what a termite looks like. But we could see the piles of dust beneath our coffee table. It looked like the floor of a carpenter's shop, the little beige mound patiently built up over the course of days. We saw similar evidence along the wooden trim in the living room. Something was clearly eating the walls, but we had no idea how to stop them. We shrugged it off. The place was a rental. We had bigger insects to fry.

Family Culicidae

The moment I saw the mosquitoes, I boiled with rage. They clung to the white plaster walls. They hovered in the air, fighting the air currents of our ceiling fan.

My blood feud with mosquitoes dates back to my earliest years. I grew up next to a swamp in New England, and spent 18 summers smacking mosquitoes off my exposed skin. I hated mosquitoes, and took great pleasure in killing them.

But Kylan had grown up in highly insulated houses in suburban Philadelphia. She had rarely seen a mosquito, much less stayed up all night while invisible insects droned into her ears.

She learned fast. The first mosquitoes were typical in every way—medium-sized, quick, persistent—and Kylan learned how to spot one and slap it dead. But then a new breed invaded our house, and they were completely different: They were tiny and dark, and they seemed to vanish in midair. They landed on us, drew blood, and then flew away without us even feeling the prick of their proboscises.

"*Look* at this," Kylan said, gesturing to her ankles and legs. If she wasn't paying attention, it took only minutes for Kylan's skin to bubble with welts. She itched fiercely. She scratched the bites until they turned bright red. She applied dollops of hydrocortisone and rubbed it angrily into her skin.

The mosquitoes flustered us, but they were also potentially dangerous: The year we arrived, Costa Rica was overrun with a Dengue fever epidemic. Thousands of people had contracted Dengue, also known as "breakbone fever," because victims feel like their skeletons are being shattered. An infection could incapacitate us for weeks or even months. Some people had died.

"What kind of mosquitoes are they?" friends asked.

"Small."

"What color?"

"Black."

"What time to they come out?"

"Mostly during the day."

"Oh," they said somberly. "Yeah, those are Dengue mosquitoes. Try not to get bitten."

Sure, we thought. *We'll try that.*

Our plight didn't surprise our friends, because they had all dealt with such pests, and far worse. Friends had seen scorpions and tarantulas and lost dogs to venomous snakes. They shrugged at our petty North American problems. We had moved to a comfy suburb in the Central Valley, where the weather was perfect. Bugs? It's the tropics. Get used to it.

But it took time. The mosquito problem came to a head when I left San José for an overnight trip to Rio Celeste. I was gone for less than 48 hours, but when I returned, Kylan had completely transformed. She had stuffed the hems of her pants into thick wool socks, which were stuffed into her toughest shoes. She wore a sweater over her shirt, and she had tucked both layers into her belt. She covered her head with a hat and her neck with a red dishtowel. She looked like a cross between a biplane pilot and a Swiss mountaineer.

"I think... I'm losing... my mind," Kylan stammered.

I knew exactly what she meant. The mosquitoes I'd faced in Vermont had broken me, just as they were now breaking Kylan. We had to do something, or else we wouldn't be able to sleep in our own home.

That Christmas, back in the States, we stocked up on repellants. The most successful brand was Herbal Armor, a non-toxic spray that smelled of citronella. It worked like a charm, and we even liked the aroma, but it felt strange squirting ourselves before bed. Meanwhile, we sealed up the windows. We never left the doors open for more than a few seconds. We scouted for any kind of standing water, where mosquitos breed. Our landlord's gardener even cleared out the gutters. Day by day, the mosquitoes vanished. As the months passed, we started to forget about them—until a mosquito appeared, and then we chased it around the house, zealous for blood.

Formicidae, *Continued*

When I saw the first winged ant flexing its wings on our kitchen wall, I advised Kylan to keep away. "I'm pretty sure they sting," I said, remembering the waspy ants of my youth. I smashed it with a sandal and tossed the carcass into the patio bushes. Out of sight, out of mind.

Then more ants appeared, waddling down from the living room skylight, looking tired as they lugged their oversized bodies in seemingly random directions. They didn't fly or attack, but their mere presence was malevolent, like a demented old man sharpening a butcher knife in the corner.

"Oh, yeah, those always come out just before a heavy rain," our friends told us.

Or they said, "You sometimes see the ants right after dark."

It sounded like folklore, but sure enough, when the ozone smelled strongest, or the sun vanished beyond the Escazú rooftops, the ants poured out of our ceiling. Behind one of the beams, we could watch a river of ants ooze along the crevice, small and large, climbing over each other in search of communal work to do. All night they scouted the floor tiles and toured the sofa cushions. We flicked them off our knees and laptop keyboards. We swept dozens of corpses into the dustbin.

The flying ants seemed like leaders at first—queens, orchestrating the hive mind—but we later saw them as bloated loners, their legs forever tangled beneath their useless bodies. When a flying ant leapt from the walls and glided to the coffee table, I was always startled, because it was airborne and could land anywhere. When it flew, I was twice as eager to crush it.

After a few months, the flying ants petered out. I wanted to feel relieved, but I had no idea why they left, nor why they'd spawned in the first place. Was it the season? The temperature? Their life cycle made no sense. Some lazy online research suggested that they were actually termite queens, but who knew? At any moment, we figured, they could come back with a vengeance.

Order Gekkota

"You will never believe what Oscar did last night," Kylan said one morning.

"What?"

"He killed a gecko."

"No!"

"Yes," Kylan said, jutting out her jaw. "And I'm *very disappointed* in him."

We had fantasized about our cats "chasing geckos," but in a playful way, the way cartoon animals might frolic in a fantasy forest. We hadn't expected Oscar, our princely ragamuffin, to pounce on a gecko, swat the tiny lizard with its claws, and then rip off its tail.

Of all the creatures we saw on a daily basis, the geckos were our favorites. Their fragile little bodies darted across the ceiling, suctioned to surfaces with their alien fingers. We had always loved geckos, ever since our first vacation together in the Dominican Republic, where geckos scurried all over our hotel, their enormous black eyes gazing back at us. We loved how they respired, their rubbery skin inflating and deflating with every breath.

How horrid to see a gecko crawl away from its severed tail, the two halves lined with blood. How awful to know that it was our cat, once so peaceful, who had gleefully disfigured it.

"I don't know where it went," Kylan said glumly. "I just feel so bad. I mean, that poor little guy. He's probably dead somewhere."

The truth was even weirder than we realized: As it turned out, Oscar had probably only scared the gecko, which had responded by *releasing its own tail*. Many reptiles have this ability, called "autotomy," enabling them to discard an appendage as a defensive maneuver. In theory, our resident gecko used his amputation to distract Oscar, then fled the scene—and he could even regenerate the tail later on.

We felt a little better.

Better, that is, until I opened the bathroom door and found the gecko, flattened inside the jamb. We had apparently squashed him while closing the door one day. I was mortified, then more mortified to have to scrape his body off the wooden frame like a wad of gum.

From then on, we scared the geckos away if they came too close. "Run!" we called to them. "Don't let the cats get you!"

The tactic didn't always work. One evening, Oscar stepped onto the back patio, which was still clear of spiders. He spotted a gecko, and before we could stop him, Oscar sucked the critter into his mouth and started to chew it.

"Oscar!" Kylan screamed.

But it was too late. The gecko crunched loudly inside Oscar's maw. Kylan looked away, horrified, but I watched as our cat swallowed deeply, then looked up, made eye contact with me, and all but smiled.

Suborder Serpentes

"What are you playing with?" Kylan whispered to Felix from across the apartment. Kylan walked slowly down the corridor, watching Felix bat the air with her paw. And then Kylan saw it. *"Oh, my God, it's a snake!"*

In all these months in Costa Rica, Kylan had astonished me with her growing appreciation for wildlife. When we first started dating, years before, Kylan had never been on a camping trip, never spent more than a few minutes in a canoe, and knew almost nothing about the natural world. Slowly, I had introduced her to the pleasures of tents and hiking trails, luring her with the promise of S'mores. But our occasional campouts in Pennsylvania had hardly prepared us for tropical living. Costa Ricans love to boast that their country is home to five percent of the world's biodiversity—which means that, if there were only 100 species on Earth, five of them would live in tiny Costa Rica. This is amazing, but it comes at a price. Yes, we wanted to see macaws and toucans, sloths and tapirs. Yes, to spot spider monkeys in their natural habitats was part of our desire to live in Costa Rica. But to see these postcard-ready animals meant that our roommates would include several more dubious species, including snakes. And Kylan had dealt with all of them, even the madness-inducing mosquitoes.

The black serpent was only a foot long, and it wriggled hysterically on the bedroom floorboards. It was Kylan who swept it into a dustpan, carried it outside, and safely deposited the snake in the street. We had felt bad about killing the spiders, which had done nothing to harm us, and we had merely chased them off ever since. Hurting a snake was unthinkable. The little guy had clearly taken a wrong turn.

But maybe not.

That night, we went to sleep as we always did. Despite recent events, we were surprisingly unconcerned about finding snakes squirming between our bed sheets. We slept deeply until after midnight, when the room started shaking. The bed vibrated beneath us, and the walls creaked.

Kylan turned toward me as the room quivered. She slapped a hand on my arm and squeezed my wrist. Then the shaking stopped. Everything was quiet.

"Hey," Kylan said drowsily. "It's an earthquake."

"Yeah," I grunted back.

"But it's over," she said. "It's okay."

Then we fell back asleep, as deeply as before.

We would later theorize that the snake was acting strangely because it sensed seismic activity. Perhaps, frightened by minute tremors in its subterranean home, the snake had headed for higher ground and slinked its way into our house. Or maybe it was a coincidence.

A few weeks later, a second snake appeared. Oscar toyed with it for only a minute before Kylan sighed, grabbed the broom, and brushed the snake into the dustpan.

"Can you take that out?" Kylan asked me, her voice flat and disinterested.

"Sure," I said.

I dumped the snake in the street.

Felis catus, Continued

Each night, the stray cat comes back. The steel panels creak as the cat stalks across our roof.

At first we didn't mind the cat. It was just an oddity, some feral creature from the neighborhood making its rounds. But Felix—our skittish little kitten—would swell with rage. Her eyes bulged; her tail puffed out. She would march the length of the apartment, following the sound of this rival cat. I never dreamed Felix could act so hostile. Our jungle cat had completed her metamorphosis, and now she was raring to fight.

When we noticed a mysterious scar on Felix's nose, we stopped letting her outside. We had heard enough catfights for one apartment: Felines routinely battled in the alleyways and rooftops, hissing and squealing. Felix was scrappy, but she wasn't an alley cat.

Now and again, the stray cat urinates on our roof. One time, when I left my shoes on the front stoop to dry, the cat pissed on them as well. The sour smell pervades the apartment for a few hours, driving Kylan insane.

"I wish we had a bee-bee gun," Kylan says. "I would shoot that goddamned cat. I really would."

I am astonished how far we've come since that first day in Costa Rica. When Adriana the real estate agent told us that we should keep our cats indoors, she added that our neighbors might try to poison them. We were shocked and appalled. What kind of psychopath would poison a cat? But now we understand. We live in the tropics now, where wildlife is bold and unapologetic. Even the walls that insulate us pulsate with organisms. We will never know the full taxonomy of our apartment, and we would probably rather not know. But I love how much tougher Kylan has become. The woman who once screamed at tiny ants can now dispose of a snake without fanfare. It's not always comfortable, but it's also no longer daunting.

"I think a gecko pooped on my pillow," says Kylan, just before we turn in. "I guess we should wash these sheets."

"Yeah," I say, yawning.

"Can you get the light?" she asks.

"Sure."

"Oh, but before you do, can you kill that mosquito?"

She points to the tiny insect on the wall.

I smile. "Absolutely."

Who Watches the Guachimán?

Every time I leave my apartment in Escazú, I pass a small security booth. The booth is small. It's just large enough for a full-grown adult to stand upright. Next to the booth, a striped traffic arm hovers above the street. When I reach the checkpoint, a man emerges from the booth, smiles, and waves.

"*¡Buenas, Robert!*" he calls. "*¿Como está? ¿Pura vida?*"

"*¡Pura vida!*" I call back.

"*¡Oh, muy bien! ¡Excelente!*"

Then a car approaches in the opposite direction, and the security guard—Santos—pushes down on a lever, which lifts up the arm and allows the car to pass through. The driver gives a half-hearted salute, and Santos salutes back.

A block farther, I stroll past the steakhouse, La Cascada. A middle-aged man with a boyish face always grimaces and nods. He doesn't wave, because his hands are always folded over his belt. Although we have never formally met, never said so much as "*buenos días,*" the man *always* acknowledges me, as if we're old buddies. Then he walks to the curb, gestures to a driver, and directs the car into a parking space.

This type of professional is called a *guachimán* (pronounced "watchee-mon"), the semi-vigilante parking guard of San José, and they're everywhere in Costa Rica. They are usually middle-aged men, sometimes old men, who wear plain clothing and reflective neon stripes. They wander the parking lot, silently waiting for cars to arrive so they can direct traffic in and out of parking spaces. They watch the car until the driver returns, and then they get a tip.

One of the perks of living in Costa Rica is that a Gringo need not drive a car. Most neighborhoods are walkable, the buses are cheap and fast, and cabs are reasonable and magically appear whenever you need them. So I don't interact much with *guachimanes*, at least not with the regularity of car commuters. But I see them everywhere, pacing around strip malls, mumbling to themselves in front of supermarkets, and even collecting tolls on public side streets.

"It doesn't matter where I park," my friend Zach told me one night, as he drove us to a holiday party. "Some *guachimán* is going to show up out of nowhere and extort me for 200 *colones*."

San José is a city without meters or standardized parking spaces, and the city is absolutely flooded with cars. Congestion is so tight that the city forbids certain license plates from driving on certain days, a practice called *restricción*. As a street map, San José looks fairly navigable—grids of numbered *calles* and *avenidas*, punctuated with parallel plazas and parks. But in practice, San José is a nightmare of battered pavement, one-way streets, steep hills, deadly switchbacks, and sloppy intersections. Highways emerge and jumble together in the most unexpected places. Drivers are aggressive, and pedestrians are daring. Every day I'm astonished I haven't seen more accidents.

That said, Costa Rica is no Bangladesh—there are crosswalks, traffic cops, and basic signage. People keep to their lanes, and most drivers at least slow down before blowing through a red light. Ticos are famously well-behaved, and few motorists drive like true maniacs. When you search for a parking space, you always know where *not* to park: "*No estacionar*" signs are stenciled right on the plaster walls. If you're desperate enough, there are plenty of *parqueos* around town, the private garages and lots of any major city.

But the *guachimanes* are also everywhere, and they say a lot about life in Costa Rica. Where official rules ebb, private guardsmen spring up. They're almost always men, and they usually lack education or skills. Many are farmers or laborers who moved to the city in search of better wages and got stuck watching parking lots for a living. A few are teenagers with no other prospects. One codger stands outside the local bank and wears a Mexican sombrero. The job isn't hard, but it's boring, and many of these guys stand around all day and night, hassling drivers and getting hassled back.

Santos isn't exactly a *guachimán*. He's more like a security guard, although he serves roughly the same purpose. Santos is charmingly overweight, with a cherubic face and bright eyes. He is almost always smiling, like a giant toddler. He is oppressively pleasant, and because I am also oppressively pleasant, we greet each other each morning with the enthusiasm of cokeheads.

"*¿Hace calor, verdad?*" I say, pointing to the sky. *It's warm out, isn't it?*

"*¡Oh, sí! ¡Muy bonito! ¡Pura vida!*" Santos sings back. *Oh, yes! Very nice! Pure life!*

Santos hails from León, a city in northern Nicaragua, and like almost every Nicaraguan I've met in Costa Rica, he's unbelievably friendly. When he's not working or chilling out at home, Santos is an eager fisherman, and he loves to cast reels in Puntarenas on his rare weekends off. With his cappuccino skin and ill-fitting uniform, Santos could easily cameo on a prime-time sitcom— the wacky neighbor, or the gawky relative with a heart of gold. He's also refreshingly honest: Before I visited Nicaragua, I asked Santos whether I should visit Managua, the capital.

"Oh, Managua!" he said, furrowing his brow. "It's very dangerous. At night, someone may rob you with a gun. I wouldn't go to Managua. You should just go to Granada." And then he closed his eyes and nodded, as if to seal the agreement.

What's funny about Santos is that he isn't much of a guard. He has no weapons, not even a whistle. He never checks drivers for ID or asks visitors' business in our *urbanización*. The security booth is a kind of placebo—when burglars see Santos, they assume our block is a gated community, even though it's not. Santos is about as effective as a scarecrow; he keeps criminals away, but he probably couldn't prevent an actual crime. Given his girth, I wonder if Santos could chase a fleeing mugger for more than a block before collapsing.

This is how many *guachimanes* are—I have no idea who hires them or how they earn their money. Do they have to train in something? Do they always ask for money, or just sometimes? Is there a standard rate, or is it negotiated on the spot? Does the *guachimán* have a union, or a club, or even the loosest social network, or do they all fly solo? Is the job even legal, or do shopkeepers just hand out undocumented cash at the end of the day?

The irony is that most *guachimanes* get hired in upper-class neighborhoods, including mine. My street would seem fairly typical in Miami or Los Angeles, but in Costa Rica, our neighbors live in the equivalent of mansions. We live near a long row of U.S. chains, like Pizza Hut and Taco Bell and Quiznos, and all of their parking lots have private security guards. Indeed, the sentry in front of our local supermarket shoulders a full-fledged shotgun—which will be handy, if a paramilitary group ever storms the organic coffee aisle.

As a full-time pedestrian, I pass my neighborhood's *guachimanes* every day, and we have a strangely warm relationship. A leathery 61-year-old named Juan often sees my wife running, and he has invited us to join him on his own jogs around town. Mikhail, who is Santos' nocturnal counterpart, is a shy Romanian with an estranged wife and child in Germany; on late nights, I often chat with Mikhail for a few minutes in German, and we trade anecdotes about our bizarre expatriate lives. Where drivers see an adversary—a crooked authority figure, a street urchin posing as a sentinel—I see fellow pedestrians. They remind me of the old men back in Pittsburgh, who spend their summers sitting on park benches and watching the traffic go by. They are fixtures of the neighborhood. In a world as cliquey and guarded as Tico culture, a nod and a wave go a long way.

"*¡Hola, Robert! ¡Robert de los Estados Unidos!*" Santos calls, like a game show host, as I return from work. The sun has melted over the rooftops and power lines, and the sky is a muddy mix of orange and storm clouds. "*¿Pura vida?*" he asks.

"*Pura vida,*" I say.

"*¡Oh, muy bien! ¡Excelente!*"

After living in Costa Rica for only a few months, I couldn't imagine Santos not there. Useful or not, he adds a human element to an otherwise impersonal suburb. If Santos were ever fired or replaced, the place would change entirely. The street would be nothing more than a street.

The Autobús Diaries

The first time I stepped onto a Costa Rican bus, I stood in the doorway like an idiot. I didn't know how much the fare cost. I didn't know what a *colón* was worth. I only knew about 20 words in Spanish, and few of them were numbers.

The driver shook his head and grimaced, then snatched the red bill from my hand. He reached into a slotted wooden box. It looked like an old-timey cash register, with its ranks of big copper coins. The driver stuffed the bill into a compartment, then sucked exact change into his palm like a vacuum cleaner. His arithmetic was instantaneous.

"*¡Gracias!*" I exclaimed, taking the coins.

"*¡Vaya, vaya, vaya!*" he commanded. *Go, go, go!*

Kylan and I sat down, shell-shocked. The bus pulled away from the airport. We were surrounded by Ticos, although we didn't know that's what the locals called themselves. We didn't know anything. We had just arrived.

These were our first five minutes in Costa Rica. Ever since that day, our life here has been tied inextricably to the city bus.

For two weeks, we lived in the town of Alajuela, and I commuted to my office in San José. If I hopped the right bus, I could arrive downtown in 35 minutes. But in those first few days, I couldn't tell one transit line from another. One morning I climbed aboard the wrong bus, and I didn't realize my mistake until we took an exit off the highway. We snaked through strange neighborhoods, climbed treacherous hills, rounded absurd corners, and narrowly missed ragged bicyclists. Tree branches raked the windows, and bundles of electrical lines loomed close.

"Excuse me," I asked the girl next to me. She was young and wore heavy eyeliner. She looked surprised to hear me speak. "Does this bus go to San José?" This was the limit of my Spanish.

"San José is the last stop," she said, smiling. "Just wait until the end."

By the time I reached downtown, the girl was gone, along with nearly all the other passengers. The ride took almost two hours.

"Keep moving!" growled an ornery old driver. "You can't stand in the doorway!"

I didn't know how to protest. He hadn't given me my change. But when I stepped into the aisle and turned around, the driver held the coins aloft, and in the oddest way: He was still sitting, but his shoulders were turned, his neck was craned, and his hand dangled between two metal bars on the side of the entrance. He dumped the coins into my cupped palm, then turned back to his steering wheel and pressed the accelerator.

I had no idea why he did that, but I didn't know how to ask, so I just sat down.

When we moved to Escazú, the Americanized suburb nicknamed "Gringolandia," my commute was cut in half. I could walk to the bus stop in five minutes, a bus would pull up almost immediately, and I'd be downtown 15 minutes later. The ride was easy and carefree. I didn't mind standing in the aisle in the early morning, because Ticos are tranquil riders. Men often give up their seats for women; youths forfeit their seats for old folks. Few riders shout into their phones or gossip boisterously in the back, as commuters had done in Pittsburgh. Day after day, the bus flew down the highway, then bumbled down sidestreets, dumping us in the park near Iglesia la Merced.

This is the Costa Rica visitors rarely see. Tourists don't take a lot of city buses. Most of them climb aboard air-conditioned vans marked "TURISMO." They have no idea where to find a *parada*, nor how much the fare costs. I didn't blame tourists for looking so anxious—literally *anxious*—to leave San José. But I also wanted them to leave. I wanted to distance myself from these clueless visitors. I liked it when they found their bus station, buried in the middle of a confusing *barrio*. I was happier when they bought their ticket and hightailed it to the nearest beach. It felt like I was no longer one of them.

When the dry season came, every bus stop smelled like piss. At first I thought it was homeless people, but then I saw them: healthy-looking men, wearing laundered clothes, pressing their bodies against concrete walls and urinating freely onto the sidewalk. Rivulets seeped between their tennis shoes and pooled against the concrete seams. Young men did this and so did middle-aged men. Sometimes a friend would act as spotter, looking both ways down the street in case a police officer showed up and cared enough to chastise them.

"I was thinking of going to San José," I said to Kylan one afternoon. "Just for some errands. You want to come?"

"*No*," she jeered. "I *never* want to go to San José. The whole city smells like pee."

The man who lumbered aboard the Escazú bus seemed to carry years of woe. He was huge and disproportioned. He wore an overlong T-shirt and his highlighted hair was mussed. A deflated backpack was slung over his sunken shoulder. He didn't sit down. Instead he stood at the front, facing all the passengers. Once the bus lurched forward, he began.

"*Buenas tardes, damas y caballeros*, and God bless you all. My name is José, and I am here because my life has been very hard. Three years ago, some men attacked me in San José, and they beat me nearly to death. I was in the hospital for many weeks, and ever since I have felt great pain. I can't walk very well, and I have bad headaches. Before the attack, I was going to medical school and wanted to be a doctor. Now I have no home and must sleep in the park…"

He held aloft what appeared to be a plastic goldfish bowl full of lollypops.

"I am selling candy in order to pay for food," he went on. "With enough money, maybe I will find a home. Please, if you have only 300 *colones*, you will help me greatly. Thank you all, and God be with you."

I saw these panhandlers all the time—men and women, all ages and shapes, who stood before the busload of people and recited their grievances in rehearsed monologues. Then they made their way down the aisle, taking coins in their hands. Sometimes they sold things, like breath mints or religious tchotchkes. Other times they simply asked for alms.

After several months in Costa Rica, I now knew enough Spanish to follow along. The performance was strange, but stranger still was that people actually dug into their pockets and handed over change. I couldn't believe how many people parted with their money, nor how easily, as if paying a second bus fare. The presentation didn't seem to bother the Tico riders. They listened quietly. No one heckled.

As in the United States, I never gave money, and the panhandlers never asked. Maybe they knew how suspicious Gringos are of homeless people, how we assume that every panhandler is a drug addict and criminal. *I* don't believe this, but I also don't hand out money. It's a policy. Watching people do so, I reconsidered.

That same week, Kylan met a physician at the hospital where she volunteered. Kylan asked about Costa Ricans handing out money to panhandlers.

"It's a Catholic thing," the physician said. "Ticos help each other out. People feel obligated to take care of each other, even strangers. Life may be really hard, but nobody starves here. People get by."

On a dry day, there was nothing more alleviating than sliding open a window. The tropical air blew across my sweaty face. I loved its cooling relief.

The opposite was also true: On a rain-drenched day, the bus was sticky with body heat, and everything smelled like damp fabric and moist shoes. Sometimes I cracked a window, but raindrops would fleck my face. There was no escaping the discomfort. Exiting the bus only meant getting soaked in the downpour.

I had rarely seen a TV on a bus before, but there it was, looming over the seats and playing videos for the amusement of passengers. The videos were short clips, probably lifted from YouTube.

The audio was muted. Some clips showed kittens jumping off counters, dogs wrestling with cats, an ostrich pecking at a man's head. Other clips showed skateboarders smashing into pavement, teenagers trying to backflip off buildings, bicyclists toppling over their handlebars. The violence was surprisingly vivid: In some clips, riders flipped their ATVs and hit the ground, looking flattened as corpses. One woman slipped on the edge of a pool and cracked her face against the concrete edge.

The company was called Móvil Media Costa Rica, a marketing group that specialized in putting videos on buses. Every clip was like "America's Funniest Home Videos," but more flagrantly destructive. Most passengers watched the footage in silence. Some cracked smiles, especially at the litter of kittens following a bouncing ball in unison.

Kylan had more problems than I did. One evening, three rowdy boys tried to catch her attention. They kept yelling, "Hey, *macha!*" to the back of her head. When she stepped off the bus, a chivalrous young man escorted her down the street and asked if she was okay. Kylan was grateful for his help, as was I. Catcalls and harassment popped up everywhere, and on the bus there was no easy escape. I was furious at those nameless hoodlums, but there was nothing I could do.

Months later, before a soccer match, a homeless man hobbled aboard and frantically blew a vuvuzela. He was old and very drunk, and he sat down next to Kylan, even though the bus was empty. He put an arm around her shoulder and blew his horn jovially. Finally he sensed her reluctance to celebrate and released her. The homeless man opened a window, aimed the vuvuzela outside, and blew blasts of sound into the street.

Kylan stepped off the bus, and as usual, the *parada* smelled like urine.

We met our friend Margarita for drinks. She is gutsy and plainspoken, and we loved hanging out with her. Because we were so often clueless, Margarita enjoyed explaining Costa Rican rituals to us.

"Okay," Kylan said. "What is up with the change thing?"

"The change thing?"

"On the bus. They hand the change over their shoulders. Like, between the bars."

"Oh, yes," Margarita said, laughing into her Imperial bottle. "It's because there's a sensor."

"A sensor?" I said, incredulous.

"Yes. Like a laser. They use it to count how many people get on and off. They don't want you to reach across it, because it will mess up the numbers."

"So," I said, "they have a laser beam that can count passengers, but they keep their money in a wooden box?"

"I know," Margarita said. "It's ridiculous."

"How about the panhandlers?" I said. "The people who tell you about their lives and then ask for money?"

"You know, they didn't exist ten years ago," Margarita said. "I never saw one before that. But then there were more and more, and now they're everywhere. I actually called my sister from the bus one time. She lives in New Jersey. In the middle of our conversation, she said, 'Hey, is that one of those people?' She made me hold up the phone so she could hear. Then she said, 'Wow! That was a good story. They've gotten really good at that.'"

On the way back from the suburbs, the rain poured so hard that I could barely see out the fogged-up windows. When I thought I had reached La Sabana Park, I slipped out the backdoor, but at the edge of the steps, I realized we were still a couple of miles short.

When I stepped back into the bus, the driver glared at me in the rearview mirror.

"Hey, you have to pay!" he called.

I moved to the front and said, "Oh, I got on before. Back in Juan Santamaría Park."

"I know," he snapped. "I remember. But you stepped off. You have to pay again."

I swelled with anger. The driver had seemed so nondescript before. Now he seemed ornery and hostile. I suddenly hated him. I understood him perfectly, and I hated him.

"Fine," I said in Spanish. "I'm getting off, then."

And before he could respond, I stomped into the rain and spread open my umbrella, creating a fabric barrier between us.

The bus drove away, and I hoped I had pissed him off. Stupid, penny-pinching driver.

When the next bus came, my clothes were moist and I had to pay the same extra fare. But I didn't care. I had never sounded aggressive in Spanish before. I thought of that first helpless ride from the airport, how far I'd come in nine months. I watched the rain slide down the windows, and my heart pounded with petty victory.

The sun was setting as the bus careened toward Escazú. It had been a long day, and I was tired. I wanted to eat and sleep, nothing else.

A skinny kid stood up and started to tell us about his life. He struggled to stand straight, because the bus was jostling through traffic. I was listening to music through my ear buds and couldn't hear him, but I saw the earnest pain on his face. At last he raised a plastic sack of candy and stumbled down the aisle. Some people gave money. Others didn't. He handed out little colored bricks, like Jolly Ranchers.

He looked like he would pass me without a word.

I handed him two coins. 150 *colones*.

"Hey, it's not much, but it's all I have," I said. It was true. I put the money in his hand. The kid bowed his head wordlessly. "Good luck," I said.

I stepped off the bus.

The air smelled sweet, like the coming of rain.

La Gente

Beach Town

I really envied the dogs.

They wandered the roads with abandon. They slept wherever they wanted. They were shaggy and street smart, and they didn't keep much of a schedule. Most dogs had no collars or licenses, and they went by several names. They'd follow us down the beach. They made a show at dinner, circling our table and eagerly eyeing our plates for scraps.

Really, the dogs set the tone for Brasilito, one of Guanacaste's most laidback beach towns. Clocks don't matter much here, nor do fences or rules. From the moment we stepped off the bus, I imagined what it would be like to live in such a place: I could set up a crab shack, talk up travelers, and scratch a stray dog's ear for a few hours a day. I'd have a boat, obviously. And maybe a motorcycle.

Kylan and I spent three days in Brasilito—a long weekend away from our rainy life in the Central Valley—but it took only a few hours to fall into its soothing rhythm. The town seemed bite-sized at first, easily digestible. But like many beach towns that have resisted large-scale development, the simple veneer was deceiving. The residents were proud. And they worried about the town's future.

My reason for visiting Brasilito was a new restaurant, Azul, which was receiving its grand opening. My editor asked me to cover it for the paper, but she also knew I wanted an excuse to bum around the beach. We stayed at Hotel Brasilito, perhaps the best-known hotel in the area. The owner was Shellay Martin, a 42-year-old New Zealander who arrived in town nine years earlier and bought the hotel from a German couple.

"How did you settle here, of all places?" I asked.

"The long way," Martin said, smirking.

Before she opened Hotel Brasilito, Martin had zigzagged all over the globe, and the decision to move to Costa Rica was methodical and meticulous. Martin had lived and traveled extensively in New Zealand, Australia, Canada and the United States, including several stints in Southern California. During a long sojourn in Los Angeles, her house exploded in value, and she sold it for a staggering profit.

"I thought, 'Where can I take the money I've got, where it's warm, I can be near the ocean, and it's politically stable?'" she recalled. Martin and her then-husband hoped to settle in Hawaii, but the high cost of living foiled their plan. So they picked Costa Rica. "I grew up on an island surrounded by the Pacific," she quipped. "I need to live near the water."

Now her 13-room hotel was doing nicely. She averaged 50% occupancy every month, which wasn't bad considering the low season's lull.

As we talked, an enormous hound wandered over and begged for food.

"*No*," Martin snapped.

The dog stared for a moment, then settled onto the floor for a nap.

"All the animals here just showed up at my doorstep," said Martin, gesturing to various cats around the dining room. "This dog belonged to the bar next door. But he got sick, so they stopped feeding him. I gave him some food and his shots. Stick a needle in him and he loves you forever. His name's Bambi. But that's no name for a dog that big."

From the main road, Brasilito looks as small as a town can be. There's one bus stop, one grassy square, a ring of shops and restaurants, and a crescent of sand. Yet this view is deceptive: Buildings line the highway for a few miles in either direction, and there's a large squatters' settlement tucked into the trees along the beach. The town is home to about 3,000 people, although a visitor would be hard pressed to find where they live. The forests and hills swallow most of the town, which is just fine as far as tourists are concerned.

On that humid October weekend, the town was practically empty. The low season is brutal to Brasilito, a town that relies on tourism to survive. Rainstorms can pour for days, so most hotel rooms are vacant, and the restaurants are mostly peppered with locals. But this is typical here. In guidebooks, Brasilito is described as "underrated," "undiscovered," and a "hidden gem." Unlike nearby Playa Flamingo, no all-inclusive resorts dominate the beachfront. There are no U.S. chains, no throbbing nightclubs, no box stores. Locals hang out in chairs and hammocks, watching the world go by. They play a pickup game of soccer in the central square every afternoon. Expats insist that the town retains its Tico identity. They say that "*pura vida*" still means something here.

The most luxurious place in Brasilito isn't exactly *in* Brasilito, but next door: Playa Conchal is a pristine white beach that sprawls sweetly around a blue inlet. While Brasilito's sand is brownish and the water is murky, Conchal is geomorphic perfection, and it's only a 10-minute stroll away. Instead of sand, Conchal's shore comprises innumerable tiny shells, which gleam brightly in the sun. The water is crystal-clear, and nary a building can be seen. Instead of high-rises, Playa Conchal is wreathed in rainforest and hills.

Gorgeous scenery aside, the town is a bargain: Our room at Hotel Brasilito cost only $49 per night, including the view of the water, AC, and a private bathroom. In the balmy heat, even the cold-water shower was refreshing. Except for a few couples and families, we had the place to ourselves. Indeed, Brasilito is only really overrun twice a year—just after Christmas and during Easter, when thousands of Costa Ricans swarm the country's beaches in search of holiday R&R. During those brief spikes, the roads are clogged with traffic jams, and hotels are overbooked months in advance. Otherwise, the town is fairly calm, even sleepy, all year round.

Which isn't always a good thing. Brasilito strikes the delicate balance of so many small tourist towns: Attract too few people, and the town collapses. Attract too many, and the town could bloat with development. Feast or famine is the rule. So far, Brasilito has remained tenuously in between.

I didn't have to spend much time in Brasilito to realize that its small-town character is sometimes uncomfortable. There's only one ATM, which often malfunctions, and there isn't a single gas station within town limits. Sidewalks are nonexistent, even on the narrow bridge into town. I found only one supermarket (if you can call it that), and most of the stores are haphazardly stocked. Meanwhile, the locals all know each other's business, and they enjoy gossip. Many of the buildings in Brasilito aren't up to code, and much of the development—especially the squatters' village—flagrantly defies the Maritime Zone Law, which prohibits construction within 200 meters from the water. Locals murmur of corruption and nepotism in the local government. Driving cars and ATVs on the beach is prohibited, but so many drivers do it that their wheels have dug an ad hoc road into the sand. Locals told that six months earlier, a horse slipped on the beach and its rider, a tourist, hit the ground and died. (Since that tragic accident, horse riders now require helmets, and riders seemed to observe the rule.)

Even the entrepreneurial spirit can get aggressive. Restaurateurs wave menus in your face and boast about the freshness of today's catch. The same teenaged equestrian will bug you to ride his horse on the beach, day after day. A mustached man may follow you down half the beach, intoning, "You would like a quad ride? Horse ride? Boat ride? Very cheap!" When you say no, he may storm off, because you're one of the only customers he'll see all day. For micro-businesses in a tiny village, you either hustle or perish. And when nearly every storefront closes shop and switches off the lights by 9 p.m., the window of opportunity isn't that big.

Although tourists will rarely see it, Brasilito has its share of serious poverty. Many families still live without basic utilities. On the bus, a frustrated Peace Corps volunteer vented to me about the abysmal school system. "There are no books," she said. "They see a computer and they don't even know how to turn it on. It's just a box to them."

Still, a large consensus is that people in Brasilito want to be left alone, especially the expats. They're phobic of regulations and committees, and they abhor large-scale construction projects. They know that the wrong kind of attention could ruin the cultural ecosystem they've created. They don't mind being an obscure point on the map, as long as enough tourists show up to keep them solvent.

The big fear is that Brasilito will morph into Tamarindo, the Gringo-heavy surfers' mecca located only 20 minutes away.

"Tamarindo is the only place in the world where I've been on the beach, with my children, and was offered cocaine," said Martin, with her customary dry humor. She remembers when she came to Costa Rica, nine years ago, and Tamarindo was a nightmare of gridlock traffic and washed out roads. (She's fond of calling the town "Scam-a-Gringo.") "The recession improved Tamarindo greatly," she added, smirking.

Each day, a bearded man rides his horse down the road, calling out, "Merry Christmas!" Everybody brought him up in conversation. "Have you met the Merry Christmas guy yet?" they asked me. "He actually wore a Santa Claus suit last December." The way they talked about him, I thought he might actually hand out presents.

Eccentrics are everywhere in Brasilito—people with unusual backgrounds, peculiar skills, bizarre habits. Three roving mariachi singers show up wherever you go. In English, their band is known as The Screaming Vagabonds, and they usually visit three or four restaurants per night, serenading tables with Spanish songs for a couple thousand *colones*. They met each other through mutual friends, and each player has strummed a guitar for 12 to 20 years. When they approached our table, the mustached guy said, "Hello, my friend, you would like a song? We are not *too* expensive." And because I chuckled, they started to play.

The most talkative expat was Javier Cantellops, an energetic, heavily tattooed 31-year-old. He had recently opened Tortugas, a small eatery on the main square, with his brother Hugh. Each time we passed the restaurant, Javier tried to engage us in conversation, and we finally relented and took a table. The menu featured a range of fish that the brothers caught themselves each morning.

"We're all the kind of people who are hard-working," said Javier, as he loomed over our table. Javier and Hugh had grown up in South Carolina, but their mother was Costa Rican and their father was Puerto Rican. After serving in the Middle East as an airborne ranger, then working as a wildlife specialist in Florida,

Javier wanted a change of pace. "The *pura vida* lifestyle isn't for everybody," he declared. "But we don't like to listen to people boss us around. After the military, I got sick of that."

Like the Cantellopses, the expats of Brasilito come from all over—the United States, Colombia, Belgium, Italy, the United Kingdom—and the only thing they have in common is a love for that tiny Gold Coast community. Somewhere along the line, they all fled hectic lives, and Guanacaste sets them free. In Brasilito, even well-to-do folks appreciate callused hands. Instead of retirees in condominiums spending their days poolside, the expats are remarkably feisty. Most people haven't finished their careers; they've just started new incarnations. Before becoming an expat, Javier served in the military, performed stunts for the film *Black Hawk Down*, and wrestled with all kinds of wild animals. (Like so many expats, Javier has a nickname, Tortuga, Spanish for "turtle"). His brother Hugo spent years as a horse trainer and show-rider, along with his wife, Gabriella. Now Hugo spearfishes every day, taking his boat into the bay and bringing fresh catch to the restaurant.

"I've had boats throughout my life," said Hugo, a drowsy-looking guy with the long blond hair of a surfer. As for his new home: "This is one of the last true Tico towns. I didn't want to move to Tamarindo. This is the furthest thing from a rat race."

The brothers' family owned a sugarcane farm in Guanacaste, and Hugo and Gabriella wanted to live close to that property. They'd been married 15 years and had two kids, but they described their life as one of routine adventure—catching fish, giving tours on the boat, smoking cigarettes in front of the new restaurant and chatting up strangers.

"This place was a shack," said Javier, pointing to his new stools and picnic tables. Until recently, the place was known as Crazy Lobster. "The health department had to shut it down, and we had to bring it up to code. We wanted to bring a blend of Costa Rican food and U.S. cuisine. Raise the bar a little bit." Javier pointed to himself. "That's the lesson of the *tortugas*: Never live in your shell forever. Always have the courage to stick your neck out."

"There are a lot of people running away from things," said Gabriella. "We have two children. We wanted them to have a better quality of life. You could say we're running away from our old life."

When we finally arrived at Azul, the entrance was subsumed in artificial mist. Every dining table was packed with couples and families, and servers whirled around the circular bar. Guests conversed and held glasses of sangría aloft in the dim orange light. Music blasted from speakers. Now and again a waiter appeared, carrying a tray of ceviche or fish tacos. The atmosphere was already festive by the time the live band started playing, and soon a group of middle-aged women hit the dance floor.

Until a couple of years ago, this restaurant was known as Happy Snapper. The bar had a lot of regulars, and one of them was Sildelau Salcedo, a hotel manager from Mexico City. Salcedo loved spending his free time at Happy Snapper. He liked the upscale tropical atmosphere, but he particularly loved its view of the water. The building was nestled across the highway and a short distance from the shore, and if he sat on the restaurant's second story, he could lovingly watch the sun set over the Pacific.

After Happy Snapper went belly-up, Salcedo bought the place with his business partner, Gerardo Brenes, a grandfatherly man and veteran politician. Salcedo wanted the new restaurant's name to reflect its oceanic locale, so he dubbed it Azul (Spanish for "blue"). Renovation work was slow, and Azul's grand opening was delayed several times. Locals told me than many other restaurants had failed to launch; many of them had no idea that Azul was opening that night.

But Salcedo beamed the entire evening, welcoming guests and embracing everyone he met. Brenes was more reserved, and he broke away from his guests to stand by the bar and survey the scene, smiling contentedly. Their expressions were the portrait of satisfaction, years of yearning finally redeemed.

As the music throbbed and dancers gyrated, a woman approached me. She was stunningly beautiful and wore an elegant cocktail dress. She said her name was Laetitia Deweer, Board President of CEPIA, a local nonprofit. She explained that CEPIA was attempting to build the first-ever community center in Guanacaste, in the nearby town of Huacas.

"We are still $100,000 short of our goal," Deweer shouted over the music. "We need to raise the money before we can even start to build it."

Deweer explained that half the students in the area drop out of high school, because they give up on classes or get pregnant. She said that domestic violence was rampant, and women especially struggled to find jobs. The new community center would have classrooms, workshops, technical equipment, and recreational facilities—if they could only raise the remaining funds.

Just then, a man barged into the conversation. He was an older U.S. expat, heavily bearded, with his denim shirt half-unbuttoned. He bellowed, "*Have you ever been fishing?*"

For a second I wondered if he was the "Merry Christmas" guy.

"Not really," I said. "Not since I was a kid."

"Well, when fish see me, they get *scared*," he growled, wincing like a buccaneer. He said he had a deal with various captains in the area, whereby he split the rental fees with willing tourists. "They don't want to pay $1,200 for a fishing trip, so I get to go for only $400," he boasted. After telling a story about "riding a shark once," he added that he often freed dolphins from commercial fishing nets, whenever he had the chance. "I don't care. I jump right in there with 'em, cut 'em loose. It's because I'm *crazy*."

He paused. I was staring. I wasn't sure what he wanted me to say, so I said nothing. He broke the silence by shaking my hand, kissing Deweer's knuckles, and skipping away to join a conga line.

Deweer and I talked for some time, and our conversation would resonate long after my wife and I left Brasilito, on a nearly empty bus bound for San José. Small as it is, Brasilito struck me as a nexus of practical dreamers. Yes, there were escapists and loners, shark-riders and screaming vagabonds, but beyond its oddball façade, people in Brasilito liked to dream big. Whether they fantasized about refurbishing a favorite bar or spearing fish or helping disadvantaged youth with their homework, the Brasilitistas were a restless bunch. They knew the odds, and they didn't care. "I'm kind of crazy," people kept saying, like a mantra. But maybe it was the right kind of crazy.

The Last War Hero

I picture it like a movie: A lanky young man crouches near the trees as the sun dwindles behind him. He wears a simple tunic, and satchel straps crisscross his chest. Around him stand older army officers in double-breasted coats and visored caps. They sigh tensely. The young man is calm but pensive. He runs his fingers through his spiked black hair—the reason his comrades call him "El Erizo," or "The Porcupine."

When someone lights a torch, El Erizo's face is illuminated in its glow, and his eyes focus on its coiling flame.

An officer says: *¿Listo?*

Listo, El Erizo echoes, and he takes the torch in a firm grasp.

Vaya con Dios, whispers an officer, and the others murmur their agreement. El Erizo nods at them individually, huffs a determined breath, and launches forward, into the gathering darkness.

He hunches over, sprints a few paces through the tufts of grass, then pauses to survey the endless turf. The air smells of smoke and burnt gunpowder. Insects sing all around. But El Erizo trains his eyes on the black barricade ahead, the wooden roof. He hears husky voices emanating from the darkness.

The young man kisses his crucifix, which hangs from a leather cord around his skinny neck. Then he springs forward, sprinting full-tilt toward the ramparts. Now he is pictured in slow motion, his face strained, lit by the streamers of fire.

Someone shouts from inside the compound. *Who goes there?* There is rustling, movement. Sentries grab their muskets from the wall. They aim, cock their weapons.

El Erizo runs faster than ever, until he is flush with the wall. He drags the flame across the roof's edge, and the thatch catches fire. Sparks fly through banners of smoke. The roof crackles and pops.

Muskets fire, blowing jets of smoke.

El Erizo is struck in the arm. He gasps, but he keeps running, spreading fire as he goes.

More shots. The lead balls fly through his uniform, and roses of blood and torn wool burst across his body. He staggers and falls, but now he is crawling through the firefight, mouth twisted in pain and defiance. He raises the torch one last time.

At the end of this imaginary movie, we never see the death-blow. But we hear the swelling violins, the passionate choir. There is a final gunshot, and then his hand lifelessly releases the torch, which falls to the ground. But the fire continues to burn as we fade to black.

That's how I picture it, anyway. Keep in mind, this is a fantasy, not a historical account. When I hear the name Juan Santamaría, this is how I envision his final hour.

Yet no biopic has ever been made about Juan Santamaría. This is shocking to me, not just because the film begs to be made, but because Juan Santamaría holds a special place in Costa Rican culture: He is the one truly famous soldier in the country's history. His triumphant sacrifice against Costa Rica's enemies took place during the only traditional war ever fought by the Costa Rican army. He is the only William Wallace, the only Ethan Allen, the only Che Guevara ever to raise arms against a clear invader and become a national legend. Other soldiers fought and died for Costa Rica, but none of them are as famous as Santamaría. He is, by the usual measure, Costa Rica's only real war hero.

When I first moved to Costa Rica with my wife, the tiny apartment in which we first lived was in Alajuela, a large town north of San José. The town is nothing to write home about: Downtown Alajuela is a dense grid of interlocked buildings, centered around the usual basilica church and urban park. The streets are narrow and the people keep to themselves. If tourists stay in Alajuela, it's only because of its proximity to the airport.

But Alajuela is also alleged to be Juan Santamaría's hometown, and because I had read about his valiant death, I was delighted to learn that Juan Santamaría Park was located just a couple of blocks from our apartment. The second we arrived, I wanted to visit the park and see the statue of Juan Santamaría, a large bronze figure that looms above the plaza.

The park itself is basically empty, except for a sheltered bus stop and some teenagers doing tricks on their skateboards. Even the statue is unassuming. Juan Santamaría is sculpted out of dark metal, and he is shown in mid-charge, holding a musket in one hand and a torch in the other. His body is hunched over and he holds his gun at his side. For a military monument, everything is wrong about it: Santamaría rides no horse, waves no sword, and doesn't even stand up straight. Yet if you know the story, it makes sense, and if you understand the pacifism of Tico culture, it's a perfect symbol. From his defensive posture, you can tell Santamaría is the underdog, an ordinary *campesino* fighting the good fight against a powerful foe. While the generals of other lands are shown commanding armies, Santamaría has only the clothes on his back. Against all odds, this teenaged drummer boy was destined to turn the tide of war. He was killed, but his courage led Central America to victory.

But victory against whom?

The Gringos, of course.

William Walker is one of the strangest characters in U.S. history, and it's no wonder high schools are reluctant to teach about him in social studies class. An eccentric lawyer from Tennessee, Walker ended up leading an expedition to Nicaragua in 1855. American adventuring in the region was fashionable in those days, and such armed entrepreneurs were called "filibusters." With a little more than 300 men, Walker waged a personal war against the local regime, overthrew the government, and named himself President of the Republic of Nicaragua.

Drunk with power, Walker promptly lost his mind: He legalized slavery and threatened to conquer other parts of Central America. Naturally, Central Americans decided to join forces against their common enemy, and Nicaraguans, Costa Ricans, and Hondurans surrounded the *filibusteros*. But Walker had conscripted some hearty mercenaries, and they successfully repelled the Central Americans for some time.

It was during the Second Battle of Rivas that Juan Santamaría allegedly volunteered to sneak into the enemy compound and set it ablaze. Caught without quarter, the *filibusteros* retreated to Granada, where Walker gave his most infamous order: He demanded that the city be burned to the ground.

Not surprisingly, the U.S. government disowned Walker as a crazy opportunist, and Central Americans remember him as a villainous invader. But not every villainous invader receives such delicious revenge: Walker skulked back to the United States, where he wrote his babbling memoirs. Then he felt restless, and soon Walker returned to Central America to tussle with Honduras. The Honduran government apprehended Walker, sentenced him to death, and executed him by firing squad in 1860. The moral: Absolute power corrupts absolutely, and then you get shot to pieces.

Walker's life is well documented, both from his own perspective and from countless others'. But Juan Santamaría was a workaday kid from a dusty Costa Rican village. In all likelihood, Santamaría was illiterate, he had never been to school, and no one had ever paid him any attention before his daring one-man assault. If you look for a book about Santamaría, you probably won't find it, in English or Spanish. (The most I found on Amazon was a coloring book. When I asked about it at Costa Rican libraries, the clerks were befuddled). Because of his humble origins, Santamaría is a folk hero in the most traditional sense— his life is a piece of oral history, a patriotic tale told from one generation to the next. Santamaría doesn't even have a gravestone to visit. It's almost as if he didn't even exist.

To get a better understanding of the Santamaría legend, I visited the Juan Santamaría Museum in downtown Alajuela. The building is a retired *comandancia*, a cross between a colonial fort and a prison, and it has become the city's cultural heart. The building has been restored to its original luster, and pristine white verandas encircle a broad court. The staff is particularly friendly, and admission is free.

I invited my friend Margarita, who lives in Alajuela, to join me on the tour. I met Margarita while writing a news story about local activists, and I had visited her Spanish poetry workshop at the Santamaría Museum, so it was only fitting we should do the tour together. When we arrived at the enormous gate, we joined about 20 young children in grade-school uniforms. They were so excited about their field trip that their chaperones struggled to wrangle them together.

The tour was clearly designed more for the children than for us: Actors dressed in historical outfits guided our group through the museum's many rooms, regaling us with stories of 19th-century politics.

"I am President Juan Rafael Mora Porras," said a man wearing a black suit and muttonchops, just like Costa Rica's early president. The children listened to his long description of Costa Rica's independence, a monologue I had difficulty following, as the words sounded like they were copied directly from an encyclopedia. The kids were remarkably attentive, but after a few minutes they got fidgety.

Suddenly a heavyset man in a white uniform jumped into the room and shouted. At the sight of a mustached *campesino* screaming at them, the kids squealed with surprise and delight. The man spoke robustly and with a cartoonish lisp. The character, it seemed, represented the "average" soldier in the Costa Rican army.

"I will march to Nicaragua to fight the *filibusteros!*" he proclaimed gruffly. But then he went quiet and turned to a cardboard cutout of a young woman in a peasant dress. "I think of my wife," murmured the soldier. "I think of my mother. I miss them dearly..."

As the only non-Tico in attendance, I couldn't help but smile at the arrival of William Walker, a mild mannered beanpole in a frock coat. He was surprisingly likeable, like a young Gregory Peck. In Spanish, his accent sounded authentically *norteamericano*, but now and again he would add some Gringo expressions, and it was clear that English was not his first language.

"I was invited here!" he exclaimed. "I am a special guest of the Costa Ricans!"

Apparently the children understood this, because they all started booing. They booed in unison, as if on cue.

"It's true! I am *a special guest!*" insisted William Walker, but the children continued to protest until they broke into giggles.

The message was straightforward: The Costa Ricans were the good guys, the *filibusteros* were the bad guys. In the fourth room, the tour's only female appeared, a big-boned woman with a robust voice. "This is a very dangerous war for Costa Rican soldiers!" she blustered. Given her passionate delivery, I decided that she was the only one of these actors I would confidently follow into battle. When she finished her speech, the actress moved toward the exit, but I flagged her down.

"I missed it," I said. "Who are you representing?"

"I'm a woman from the era," she whispered, then smiled warmly and slipped out.

(No woman in particular. She was just any Costa Rican female living in the mid-1800s. But I supposed it made sense, given that women weren't allowed to vote in Costa Rica until 1949.)

As we moved through the museum, each room displayed more uniforms, weapons, and dioramas than the last. Tiny soldiers stood in formation in recreated battlefields. A large map showed the "Vía del Tránsito," the long march from Alajuela to the San Juan River, then the boat trip to Lake Nicaragua. One display showed a battle between the Costa Rican army and an indigenous tribe. It hadn't occurred to me how far the militia had to travel, and through such difficult terrain: In order even to reach Rivas, they marched through the Costa Rican highlands, cloud forests, and jungle, lugging all their gear with them. The mules and oxen they brought were probably as frustrating as they were necessary. On the map, the Vía del Tránsito doesn't seem very long, but Central American geography is deceptive. You can never trek too far without running into a ravine or volcano.

I grew up in New England, and such historical sites are in my bloodstream. (When my Dad retired early, he started to work for the local Maritime Museum, where he still does blacksmithing demonstrations and other chores.) The Juan Santamaría Museum was familiar, as was this kind of tour.

But one thing surprised me: The tour was *boring*. And why should that be? The fight against the *filibusteros* was the closest thing Costa Rica has ever had to a serious international conflict. The museum contained flintlock pistols and cavalry sabers, uniforms and original cannon. Walker was a violent man, and he had personally fought alongside his mercenaries. This tour should be riveting. Instead, it was all lecture. The actors recited names and dates, locations and events, but there was no action at all. For a story about megalomania and tropical warfare, the recreation was stultifying.

Still, the kids seemed to enjoy it.

"I am the conqueror!" William Walker proclaimed in jovial Spanish.

"No!" the children cried.

"Who is coming to fight me?"

"¡*Nosotros!*" the children called.

"*Who* is coming to fight me?"

"WE ARE!"

Then Walker paused thoughtfully, leaned toward the children, and started to sing "Yankee Doodle." The children started to boo again. As Walker sang "riding on a pony" in his stilted Gringo accent, the children booed louder.

I laughed along with this, enjoying the show of patriotism. But I had seen enough.

"You want to get something to eat?" I asked Margarita.

"Sounds good," she said. We bowed out of the museum and headed across the courtyard, where Margarita mumbled, "We hear this so many times. I don't remember everything, but I know the basics. When I was a kid, they told the story over and over, and you just get tired of it."

We grabbed lunch at a hole-in-the-wall Caribbean restaurant down the street. As we gobbled our mounds of coconut rice, Margarita shook her head at the Santamaría story.

"You know the statue in the park?" she said. "It was based on a Haitian soldier. You see the uniform he's wearing? It's French. Our soldiers didn't have uniforms. They probably didn't even have shoes. And the Haitian guy it was based on? He was black. That's a black soldier standing in the park. And Juan Santamaría obviously wasn't black."

Part of what I like about Margarita is her no-nonsense delivery, and I knew she would have some opinions about Costa Rica's only war hero. I asked her what she thought of the legend.

"There are so many theories," Margarita said. "Some people say he was Nicaraguan. Some people say he didn't exist. It's not like there's any documentation. Some people even say that he was killed by his own side—the officers forced him to go, and when he tried to run back, they shot at him."

Margarita is young, and she has a punk-rock personality. She loves to get riled up about politics, and she has no qualms about questioning an undocumented military myth. This attitude is common among the younger Ticos I've met—they think of Juan Santamaría as just a story, a historical footnote, and not very relevant to contemporary Costa Rican life. It's hard to feel strongly about fighting Yankee Imperialism when the country boasts more than 50 McDonald's restaurants. Indeed, Margarita herself has worked for U.S. companies Hewlett-Packard and Experian. The Filibusters may have lost their war, but Gringo influence is all but ubiquitous here. So what does a 19th-Century drummer boy mean to Costa Rica? Why should Juan Santamaría matter to anybody?

After two months of living in Costa Rica, I had an epiphany.

I was passing through the National Museum in San José, and I stumbled into an exhibit called "¡Vivamos la Democracia!" The exhibit was well put together, including old documents, photographs, and other artifacts. Basically, "Democracia" was a celebration of civics. Smiley cartoon characters lined the walls, demonstrating the voting process. I read some plaques about the civil rights movement in Costa Rica, about women's suffrage, and about major changes to national laws. But I felt that something was missing.

Then it struck me: *The timeline had no wars.*

The omission shocked me, because I had never really seen a national history without armed struggle. Indeed, most of the memorable dates in U.S. history are also our bloodiest: 1776, 1812, 1864, and 1941 are recognizable to almost any high school graduate. Most U.S. students know the significance of December 7, and almost everyone on the planet shudders at the date September 11. Dates aside, violence has helped define the "American character":

My parents are part of the "Vietnam generation," and they all remember what they were doing when John F. Kennedy was assassinated. People in the United States are intensely aware of the nation's military and nuclear capabilities. Terrorism has haunted us for more than 40 years. All of us know at least one veteran, and probably scores of veterans. War is just a part of our daily existence.

Like all U.S. citizens, I grew up with war. I was only 10 years old when the U.S. invaded Panama. Operation Just Cause (as it was officially known) was the first armed conflict I personally remember. Eight months later, the Gulf War broke out. The Battle of Mogadishu unfolded in 1993; the U.S. entered the Balkans conflict in the mid-1990s; then President Clinton blew up the Al Shifa pharmaceuticals factory in 1998. All this occurred in a time of relative peace, back when the invasions of Iraq and Afghanistan would have seemed unthinkable.

Militarily speaking, Costa Rica is the polar opposite. President José Figueres Ferrer disbanded the army in 1948. Since then, Costa Rica has enjoyed more than six decades of peace. The only problem Costa Rica has faced is an ongoing border feud with Nicaragua, but neither side has fired a single shot. Given the country's geography, this is shocking: Every other Central American country has endured widespread violence, whether by dictator or drug cartel or full-blown civil war.

In a way, this tranquility could summarize the entire history of Costa Rica; all Ticos have ever wanted was to be left alone, and they have basically succeeded. The Mexican Empire couldn't govern them effectively, and the Central American Republic was too disorganized to maintain control. Since its independence in 1848, the country has experienced only a handful of coups, and the body counts were always low. The Costa Rican Civil War lasted 44 days in 1948, and only 2,000 people died. (No one knows how many casualties resulted from the Nicaraguan Revolution, but historians estimate around 30,000. The Salvadoran Civil War was even bloodier: 80,000 killed and 8,000 "disappeared," plus the 500,000 who fled the country altogether.)

As Tico friends would later remind me, Costa Rica is full of heroes, from artists and suffragettes to statesmen and soccer legends. Prowess on the battlefield may equal heroism in many cultures, but Figueres is heroic because he made battle prowess irrelevant.

To your average Gringo (or Frenchman, or Chinese), history without war doesn't even compute. It's like explaining veganism to a cattle rancher. But that absence inspires me. Indeed, it is part of the reason I'm here.

"Did Juan Santamaría exist?" read a headline in *La Nación*, Costa Rica's newspaper of record, in 2008. Historian Iván Molina Jiménez dissected the legend and its known facts in a long article for the paper, and its publication was timed to coincide with Juan Santamaría Day, celebrated annually on April 11. Molina concluded that Santamaría "was present at the battle of Rivas." He added, somewhat aggressively: "The fact that doubt is still cast on the existence of Juan Santamaría, his role in burning the barracks, and his death from such an act reveals in part the lack of historiographical debate and its progress. Also in part, these questions indicate the persistence of entrenched prejudice against oral traditions of popular origin as a source of knowledge."

From what I can tell, Costa Ricans *want* Juan Santamaría to exist, not because Ticos love war stories, but as an expression of their courage. Santamaría's sacrifice is evidence that Costa Rica can fight for its peace and progress but chooses not to. Ticos have tasted war, and now they want nothing more to do with it. End of story.

Perhaps this also explains why no one has ever made an epic film of Santamaría's life: The more you prod a legend, the more people scrutinize it. Why mess with a good thing, when Costa Rica has been so fortunate? Why celebrate war when Ticos obviously loathe it? Whether Costa Rica has "earned" its prosperity or not, the culture's disdain for violence is among its most wondrous virtues. All over the world, people look to Costa Rica as a beacon of hope, the one place where ongoing peace is possible. There is no reason to glorify Santamaría or to dwell on his exploits. Kids learn the story, and then they move on with their *pura vida* lives. In the end, it doesn't really matter whether El Erizo actually walked the earth and torched the enemy camp. Santamaría is like Robin Hood and David Crockett. No one needs details. The tale is good enough.

City by the Sea

The owner of a *pescadería* invited us to sit down on his bench. "Have a seat!" he exclaimed. "Drink a beer! Relax!"

The bench was made of metal, and it was hard on the thighs, but on a hot and humid day in the Caribbean port city of Limón, it's always nice to take a load off. My friend Beto and I clinked Imperial bottles and drank liberally. Antonio, a squinty old man with jagged teeth, grilled me about my origins.

"The United States!" exclaimed Antonio. "I lived in Miami for 30 years!" He started spurting a bunch of facts about American football, about long-retired players and favorite games. He loved living in Miami. He still had family there and in other cities across the U.S. When I asked Antonio when he came back to Costa Rica, he misheard and thought I asked *why* he came back. He shrugged his shoulders, scowled, and said, "Life happens, you know?"

"Are you from Limón originally?" I asked.

"I was born here!" he proclaimed, punching his chest. He leaned in and growled, "And *I'll die here!*" Then he burst into a piratical laugh.

It was noon on the last day of the Carnavales de Limón, one of the biggest annual parties in Costa Rica, and we had just finished lunch at the *cevichería* next door. Antonio's little fish market was a flurry of activity—mongers grabbed whole fish from packed ice, random men moved behind the counter, *taxistas* leaned against their cars in front, and everybody talked quickly and loudly in a mix of Spanish and patois.

A beefy man strode past the glass case full of fish, headed for the street, but then he whirled around and grabbed Antonio's shoulder.

"Do not trust this man!" he roared in English. "He is a—what do you call it? ¿*Un ladrón?*"

"A thief?" said Beto.

"Yes! This man is a thief!"

The entire *pescadería* exploded with laughter, including Antonio. It was the deep-throated laughter that only a bunch of old men can pull off, and only after they have been friends for years and years. It reminded me of Pittsburgh—all the craggy steelworkers in the dive bars, lounging in lawn chairs on the sidewalk, waiting for a haircut in an old-timey barbershop. It was the roughhousing atmosphere of aged testosterone, deep within a port city full of cranes and shipping containers. Years from now, when I remember 2014 in Limón, I will remember these men. I will remember how they begged us to have a second beer and kill some time with them.

"I never loved anyone," said the beefy man. "But I love rum. Rum is the only thing that never betrayed me."

Again, a burst of laughter.

That day felt like any other day in a blue-collar town. The men betrayed no anxiety about the Moín Port project, the billion-dollar renovation that had divided the city for the previous three presidencies. They said nothing about the high-profile trial of the men accused of murdering local environmentalist Jairo Mora, which was scheduled to take place within the fortnight. They didn't even mention Carnaval, which had been raging around them for eight days.

"Did you go to the parade yesterday?" I asked Antonio.

"The what?"

"The parade? For Carnaval?"

He scoffed. His lips actually flapped as he blew irritated air through them. "I don't care about that. That's not for me." And then he said the same refrain I'd heard a hundred times before: "*It's too dangerous.*"

I wanted to see Limón during Carnaval, but after a series of miscommunications, I ended up arriving on Sunday—twenty-four hours after the parade, the drummers, the feathered dancers, the big open-air concerts, and all the most voracious partying. By the time my bus arrived at the Limón terminal at 9:30 a.m., the city was clearly in recovery. Folks in the street had the dazed look of Mardi Gras survivors.

But downtown Limón was also dense with open-air markets, a vast bazaar of interlocked tents and kiosks, where merchants sold high-heeled shoes, floral dresses, fedoras, used TV remotes, plush toys, lingerie of all varieties, "*pura vida*" T-shirts, and thousands of other items. Women barbequed skewers of chicken on street corners, their faces lost in clouds of smoke. Most peculiar of all were the merchants—mostly older women—selling random wares out of grocery carts. One grandmother spread out her items on a bed sheet, where a toddler sucked his thumb and watched armies of shoppers march by.

At one end of the long street, the sidewalk was crammed with wood furniture. Rocking chairs shared space with deck chairs and tables and stools and loveseats.

"Where did all this come from?" I asked a merchant.

He was perched atop a stool and looked pleasantly surprised by the question. "Nicaragua!" he said proudly. "Most of it was made in Masaya. We shipped them all down last week, for the beginning of Carnaval. Whatever we don't sell, we have to take back."

This was only half the problem, he admitted: Aside from the sea of unsold items, the import taxes had been brutally expensive, which had ruined much of their profits. Everyone I talked with agreed that the first weekend of Carnaval was extremely well trafficked, but this weekend had been a bust. The parade had not attracted the same throttling crowds as past years. "You should have come last weekend," people told us.

Beto and I had missed the parade, but I didn't care. Ever since I moved to Costa Rica, I had looked for the excuse to hang in out Puerto Limón. Sure, we had missed the party, but we got to see the city as it settled back into its usual routine. This was the in-between period, the day that hotels emptied and hung-over tourists fled the city for parts unknown. They had eaten their fill of rice and beans. They had taken all the pictures and bought all the keepsakes they needed. Most of Limón's actual stores were closed, their garage doors sealed shut. The street venders looked tired and bored. Nearly everyone on the street seemed eager to head home.

Yet I loved having a full day and night to explore the town. Of all the big destinations in Costa Rica, Puerto Limón is the forbidden city. Given the chance, most travelers skip Limón entirely. It is a place to transfer buses, stop for directions, visit a gas station. But I had to see it. And with so many changes on the horizon, now was the time to go.

I invited my friend Alberto (affectionately known as "Beto"), a staff photographer for *The Tico Times* and one of my favorite traveling companions. Beto grew up in Costa Rica and is a Carnaval veteran; he had photographed the parade before. He knew the layout of the town and what to expect there. For Beto, visiting Limón was a chance to escape San José and enjoy some Caribbean breezes.

But Beto has a longtime relationship with the city: When he was a kid, his parents would take him on road trips, and one of the requisite stops was Puerto Limón.

"It was a little strange," Beto recalled to me over lunch. "But my Dad really likes history, so we came here a lot."

Indeed, the history is palpable. Limón is a weather-beaten place, and nearly every surface could use a fresh coat of paint, including the pedestrian walkway in the middle of town. But if you look past the bundled electrical lines and piles of litter, you'll see an old town that is shockingly well preserved. You can still discern the antique architecture along its wide streets. The gridded blocks and ample sidewalks have changed little since the days of the United Fruit Company. The ornate post office in the middle of town is nationally famous, having processed mail from 1911 to 1981. In 2012, the government began an ambitious renovation project to transform the stately old building into the official Limón Museum.

An enormous church stands on the western part of downtown, a concrete structure with a single gray turret jutting sternly into the sky. At first glance, The Sacred Heart of Jesus Cathedral isn't much to look at; the architecture is downright Soviet. But the church looks more attractive upon closer inspection, and the interior—with its ribbed wood ceiling and sprawling stained glass windows—is surprisingly beautiful. Above the altar hangs a provocative sculpture: There are three human figures, one embossed passively in the wall, a second that seems to have stepped away from the wall, and a third ascending into the air. The sculpture probably refers to Jesus Christ, but the last figure also outstretches his arms, as if newly liberated from bondage. It seems no coincidence that the figures' "skin" is dark.

One of the largest and most famous buildings is named after the Black Star Line, the ill-fated Pan-African shipping company created by Jamaican entrepreneur Marcus Garvey in 1919. Garvey had hoped to connect black business owners around the world with a steady flow of maritime commerce; he even dreamed of helping ethnic Africans resettle in Africa. He was particularly beholden to Limón, where he had worked as a timekeeper for United Fruit in 1910. Like much of Limón's history, the Black Star Line building is a monument to tragedy: The U.S. government charged Garvey with mail fraud (he advertised a ship he did not yet own), and the company disintegrated. Afro-Caribbean people who had imagined returning to the land of their forefathers never had the chance.

Since its founding, Limón has been the crucible of Costa Rica. In the 1870s, immigrants arrived from Jamaica to build a railroad from Limón's peninsula to San José. Despite their toil, the workers themselves were segregated from the rest of the country. They were forced to speak Spanish instead of their native English and patois, and the fact that their language survives at all is a testament to their resilience. When the train system was abandoned and dismantled in the 1990s, it was an affront to all that backbreaking labor.

Ever since I arrived in Costa Rica, friends have related sad stories about Puerto Limón. A bike trail along the coast was never completed. Thoughtful renovation projects never took off. "Narco" drug trafficking plagues the region, a problem mentioned by nearly everyone I met during my stay. The vocabulary is always the same: Limón has been "abandoned" by San José, "forgotten" by the rest of the country, "failed" by a useless local government and combative trade unions. The place is "dangerous," and you have to "be careful" and "watch your belongings." The caution is appreciated but exhausting.

"But I feel like Limón has so much potential," I told an expat friend a few weeks before my visit.

"They've been saying that for years," he grumbled.

Still, having lived for many years in the Rust Belt, I have enormous affection for cities like Limón. I don't mean sympathy. I actually feel more at home in second-tier cities, and I have a passionate, bleeding-heart desire to see them recover. Limón reminds me of Cleveland, that rundown industrial town that could blossom at any second (and already has, as evidenced by its Ohio City district). If Limón had just one successful *barrio*—even one thriving street—I am convinced the city would radically transform in a matter of years.

The danger, of course, is gentrification. If a few feisty investors dump a bunch of money into trendy businesses, a handful of daring millionaires could buy up all the old buildings and repurpose them as luxury lofts, driving out the current residents. Today it seems far-fetched, but it's happened hundreds of times around the world. Some of the most fashionable neighborhoods in U.S. cities were once crime-infested slums. Limón is a ripe fruit.

At the gates of the port, we flashed our press badges and the security guards let us in. We made our way into the main marketplace, where local merchants sold knickknacks to tourists. Unlike the Carnaval market, these tables were laden with regular souvenirs: bags of coffee, paintings of toucans, carved wooden bowls, floppy hats with "Costa Rica" written in green, all the usual stuff.

A young woman was offering massages. She was plump and bespectacled, like a bookish Queen Latifah. She said she had grown up in Puerto Viejo, but she now lived and worked in Limón.

"What do you think of Limón?" I asked.

"What do you mean?"

"What's unique about the city? What makes it special?"

She shrugged, as if I had asked her an impossible riddle. "It's fine," she said. "But I wouldn't live here if I didn't have a job. I'd rather be back in Puerto Viejo. I miss being there."

Beto and I made our way outside, crossed the broad parking lot beneath a baking sun, and ambled toward a docked cruise ship.

I once spent three months on a ship, and I know what it's like to spot land after a few dizzying days at sea. But what do cruise passengers see when they arrive at Limón? I turned around and tried to see the city through their eyes. The portside buildings are low and lined with rust. The sign that reads "*Bienvenidos/ Welcome*" looks old and scoured. When you drive along the coast and skirt Limón's airport, the vista is breathtaking; cargo ships rest in a drowsy haze. But looking in the opposite direction, the landscape isn't as impressive. The rolling hills are too distant to make much of an impression. Indeed, it's hard to tell what you're even looking at.

Limón handles about 80 percent of Costa Rica's foreign trade. What does that mean? If you visit a San José supermarket and buy five items, four of them came through this port. Those items were packed into a cargo container. The container arrived by ship, it was lifted into the air by an industrial crane, it was fitted onto a truck, and the truck drove that container to that very store.

Port cities are rough by nature. They absorb an endless influx of mariners and their cargo. They must house and feed and entertain those sailors, who spend weeks and months surrounded by water. No one has ever successfully turned Limón into anything but a port city. The community is stripped to its barest essentials—warehouses, stores, restaurants, a couple of hotels, and an unusually prominent cemetery, where the aboveground tombs gleam like ivory. Where other Costa Rican communities have reinvented themselves as tourist meccas, Limón has just gotten more dog-eared. It is what it is.

What do those tourists see, when they head down the gangplank and set foot on Costa Rican asphalt? Until now, not much.

Beto and I took a siesta at the Park Hotel, then ventured back out for dinner. As we descended the hotel's steps to the first floor, the large plate-glass windows opened onto the sea, which was tinted pink and purple with the vanishing sun. A few people were examining menus in the hotel's restaurant, but otherwise it felt like we had our run of the place.

What is striking about Limón is its diversity. Like Avenida Central in San José, the streets are a rainbow of different skin tones, heights, builds, ages, and mannerisms. While Limón is most famous for its Afro-Caribbean culture, the city is packed with Chinese-owned shops and restaurants. We ended up with plates of chop suey in a dimly lit eatery.

"*¡Con mucho gusto!*" chortled the cherubic waitress as she set down our plates. She smiled sweetly and headed for the kitchen.

Everyone we had met was friendly. The Caribbean is usually described as "relaxed," but this was something more—people went out of their way to give us directions and ask us questions. No one minded that we took photos of everything we saw, and some people even posed, giving us thumbs up or crossing arms like tough guys. Men had passed me all day and called out phrases in English—over-pronouncing "How are *you*, my *friend?*" as if to prove their command of the language.

As the night thickened, the streets swelled with activity. During the day, the long avenues had been subdued, yet now they pulsed with traffic, shouting vendors, teenagers meandering in packs, couples making out in the doorways, preteens dodging cars in the street. Music pounded from second-story windows; bass vibrated through passing SUVs. I wanted to preserve this moment, to somehow bottle this bit of history. The city was on the cusp of enormous changes. A week after our stay, local unions would protest the Moín Port project, and 68 people would be arrested. Soon after that, Limón would host a trial for the suspected murderers of Jairo Mora, the controversial environmental activist. It was impossible to gauge what would happen to the city, how the Moín Port would be restructured, whether downtown Limón would be renovated, whether daily life would radically transform—or would it change at all? More than any other place in Costa Rica, Limón's future always seems uncertain, and the city has endured so many disappointments that locals seemed resigned to wait and see what happens.

When we retired to our hotel, Beto and I grabbed a nightcap and talked about the city. We had loved our time walking around. For all its problems, Limón is down-to-earth. Friends had warned us of pickpockets and mugging, but we hadn't once felt unsafe. The only thing the city seemed to lack was something to do, some reason to come back. I sipped rum—remembering what that man had said earlier, how it was the only thing that had never betrayed him—and looked through the window, at the stone wall that lined the Caribbean sea, where couples cuddled beneath street lamps.

"Pardon me!" came a voice.

We swiveled toward a disheveled man, his face scruffily bearded and the skin of his naked arms blemished. He leaned over our table and extended a hand.

"How are you, my friend? You speak English?"

The scene was confusing: The man's clothes were mismatched; bits of debris were stuck in his hair, and his expression was frantic and wide-eyed. Yet he stood in a fine dining room, surrounded by starched tablecloths and folded napkins.

"Sir, maybe you could help me, please…" he stuttered.

Before he said another word—before Beto or I could say anything—the hotel's security guard appeared. The guard had a barrel chest and bulbous biceps. His face was stone-serious. He clapped a hand on the bearded man's shoulder and whirled him around. He growled to the bearded man in threatening Spanish and half-guided, half-shoved him toward the lobby. The man protested meekly, but he knew the jig was up. A second later, the bearded man staggered into the street, and the security guard locked the glass door. They glared at each other through the transparent wall that divided them.

We were sealed inside the hotel now. We could see the dark streets through the walls of windows, but all the entrances were bolted. I felt trapped inside an enormous goldfish bowl. Unlike most buildings in San José, the Park Hotel has no wrought iron bars that encage it, but it was still clear that we were outsiders, and these walls were supposed to protect us from the city. Out there, Carnaval was ending. And the fate of the city? Only time would tell.

Day of the Devils

The bull wagged its head side to side. Its feet dragged in the dirt. Men yelled and chanted. They jumped up and down. They thrust their pelvises. They danced in circles, taunting the bull with their shrieks. They whipped at the bull with rubber hoses and colored tassels.

Suddenly the bull launched forward. It slammed its head into a mustached man and pushed him backward. At first I thought the high bushes would stop them, but the man crashed through the shrubbery, somersaulting off a muddy ledge. His body thumped hard as he hit the bottom of a drainage ditch, his limbs flailing all around. More men ran to him, grabbing his wrists and pulling him to his feet.

Wow, I thought. *This is a lot more intense than I thought.*

The "bull" was not an actual bull, but a body-puppet made of burlap sheets. It didn't look like a bovine animal so much as a boxy tent, but the wooden mask of a bull was affixed to the front, and a makeshift tail wagged in the back. Every few minutes, the man inside the abstract bull would tip the contraption over and climb out, and another man would replace him. Then began a new round of gibing and charging.

As the bull whirled in random directions, the crowd of spectators backed away. The bull might charge at anyone; no one was exempt.

My wife Kylan stood nearby, her brow furrowed. She turned to our guide, Pedro Rojas. "Is that normal?" she whispered.

"Oh, yes," said Pedro.

Kylan leaned toward me. "Maybe watch your camera. This looks like it can get pretty rough."

This was the *Juego de los Diablitos*, or Little Devils' Game, a communal ritual that takes place each year in the Boruca

Indigenous Reserve. For 400 years, the Brunca people have donned masks and constructed their bull. Their strange combat is more than mere horseplay; the bull represents the Spanish conquistadors, who arrived in the 16th century with swords, muskets, and a mission to enslave anyone they found in the unmapped rainforest. The masked men represent the Brunca people, fighting back against the invaders.

After long minutes of roughhousing, two of the men lifted conch shells to their lips and blew long and hard. Slowly, the combatants stepped away from the bull, lifting their masks like football helmets and wiping their brows. They sauntered away from the grassy yard, entering the main road, where they ambled toward the next battlefield. Over the course of the day, the group would visit nearly every household in the village.

I first saw a Brunca mask in an Alajuela gift shop called Verdes y Colores. The mask was shaped like a devil, and its twisted fangs and horns were so monstrous that I actually laughed aloud. Its mouth snarled and a tongue lobbed out. I didn't realize that the mask was carved out of a single piece of balsa or cedar, then meticulously painted in vibrant colors. It never occurred to me that someone might actually *wear* the mask.

"The Brunca wore the masks to scare off the Spaniards," said the store's clerk, María, who has since become a good friend. "The Spanish were Catholic, and the masks looked like devils, so they were afraid to fight."

I smirked at this. *Silly, superstitious conquistadors*, I thought.

After that day, I saw Brunca masks everywhere. Scores of them hung in souvenir shops at Juan Santamaría Airport. Dozens more covered the walls of commercial galleries in downtown San José. With closer inspection, my appreciation grew. The masks were startlingly imaginative and detailed; some represented a single jaguar or monkey, but others showed toucans in trees, eyes peering through foliage, waterfalls pouring past humanoid mouths. They were not merely faces, but three-dimensional landscape portraits, a mix of tropical scenery and beastly visage. I had never seen anything like it before.

I started to give Brunca masks as Christmas gifts, because I admired the craftsmanship and I knew that each mask was unique. But I wanted to see where these masks came from. I had heard about the *Juego*, and I had a vague notion what the ritual looked like. The Culture Ministry dispatches dozens of press releases every December in the hopes that the media will attend the event. I had seen the overexposed digital photos that the ministry had sent, showing disheveled men in costumes. But what was it really like to be there? I had to see it for myself.

Luckily, I wasn't alone.

"I've always wanted to see it," said my friend Lindsay, a fellow writer for *The Tico Times*. "I miss it every time, and I really want to go this year."

Kylan and I decided to make a road trip out of it, and Lindsay offered to chauffeur, since her car is equipped with four-wheel drive. For a San José resident, Boruca is fairly far afield. You can't just hop a bus from the Coca-Cola bus terminal, nor is there a standard shuttle service. To reach Boruca, a traveler must drive through the mountains of central Costa Rica, rising to ear-popping elevations, then descend the hair-raising curves of the Pan-American Highway. The scenery is spectacular: Mythic ranges scroll past the windows, along with valleys draped in clouds. As we drove, the road leveled out past San Isidro, and the rainforest was subsumed in darkness. When we turned off the two-lane highway, we bumbled along a dirt road, losing ourselves in the dark hills. The road became rockier, more potholed. Lindsay's Tracker jostled its way through the night, until we descended into Boruca's valley.

We met Pedro at the central church, where a 10-meter cross rose from the gravel parking lot into the navy blue sky. Scattered lights ringed the vale. We could barely make out the wooded hills that surrounded us. Pedro arrived on foot, a big man with bright eyes.

"*Buenas noches*," said Pedro in a soft bass. "*¡Bienvenidos a Boruca!*"

I had no idea what to expect in the "Boruca Indigenous Reserve," an official title that didn't conjure any images. Centuries ago, the Brunca lived in conical huts, whose thatched roofs reached to the ground. Without pictures or descriptions, I resorted to this pre-Columbian portrait: pigs hanging from spits, *caciques* wearing gold plates in their ears, and massive stone spheres standing in the grass. These were the images I had gathered from dioramas in the Jade Museum and Gold Museum in San José. The last time anyone had lived like this, Cervantes was still writing *Don Quixote*.

When we stepped out of our cozy *cabina*, I was surprised how the village appeared in morning light: Stout concrete cottages stood in rows on the sloped dirt roads. Nearly all the houses were single-story and small, but they seemed well-constructed and cared for. A chorus of roosters had called all night, and they continued to vocalize long after dawn. Pedro led us past a modern *pulpería* stocked with regular groceries. Painted wooden signs advertised rugged souvenir shops. We arrived at a small *soda* and sat at a plastic table in the front yard. The village was a maze of roads that went in all directions, snaking up hills and dropping into forest, but in general Boruca looked like almost any other small town in Costa Rica.

As we gobbled our *gallo pinto* and tamales, Pedro folded his hands on the table. "Do you have any questions?" he asked.

"First off," I said, "I've always been curious: Are the people called the Boruca, or the Brunca?"

Pedro took a deep breath and looked upward. He did this every time we asked a question, as if preparing the perfect response. At last he murmured, "The people are called the Brunca, but this reserve is called Boruca."

I sighed contentedly. For more than a year, I had heard various people—mostly white, mostly from the United States—bicker about what the Brunca call themselves. A few letters might not matter to most people, but I wanted to know for sure. We all know that European colonists spent centuries misnaming the indigenous people of the Americas. Using the right name, even the butchered, Romanized version of the right name, feels significant. Saying "Lakota" instead of "Sioux" will never bring back the dead of Wounded Knee, but it's a shot at common decency.

But vocabulary is also a touchy subject, because the Brunca language is critically endangered. As Pedro explained it, only a handful of elders remember the ancestral tongue, and when they die, so too will their idiom. Unlike the Mayan languages of Guatemala or the Guarani languages of the Amazon, which are still spoken by thousands of everyday people, Brunca may have no future. While bilingual signs are posted around the shops, showing phrases in Brunca and Spanish, these are only novelties. There are no libraries full of Brunca-language books or a radio station broadcasting Brunca-language conversation. Like hundreds of languages around the world, Brunca teeters on the brink of extinction.

Lindsay and I tag-teamed Pedro with questions. After each query, he paused, considered fully, and then spoke in a slow, uninterrupted monologue for up to 10 minutes. He said about 2,500 people lived in the village, more than we had expected. (According to some sources, only 2,000 Brunca exist at all, including both the Boruca reserve and its sister community, Rey Curré.) Pedro listed the crops that area farmers grew—mostly beans, corn, and coffee, among other tropical staples. Pedro himself has lived in this village his entire life, working mostly as a car mechanic.

Our last coffee slurped, we followed Pedro around the corner to a small workshop. Inside, a craftsman sat in a chair and nodded to us. In his lap he cradled a wooden mask, half-carved, which he was patiently sculpting with a chisel. The mask was not yet painted, but the facial features were already clear.

I watched, reverent, as the man whittled. He leaned over his work, concentrating on the curls of wood that floated to the floor. This was exactly what I had hoped to see. It looked so normal, here in Boruca, to see a man shaping a block of wood into a sacred mask. As Lindsay snapped photos, I peered outside at a commons area, where a dozen Brunca sat on benches and steps. Women braided each other's hair. The children and mothers sat snugly together, gazing in all directions. No one stirred. This little patch of ground, wedged between some squat buildings, might as well have been their living room.

"Look at them," whispered Kylan. "It really *looks* like a community."

This was the difference between my small hometown in Vermont, which has even fewer people than Boruca, and an indigenous village: Where Vermonters are private people, giving each other space, the Brunca are the last vestiges of an ethnic group, and they have always clung to each other for survival. Despite Spanish conquest and Catholic conversion, the Brunca behave like one big family. For the rest of our stay, we saw people clustered intimately together. I didn't want to generalize or presume. We were only visitors. But the closeness was palpable.

For hours, we followed the bull from house to house, and the battle continued. Drummers drummed, pipers blew shells, the masked men jeered and the bull charged. The fighting got rougher as we went; at one point, the bull slammed into a cluster of onlookers, pushing some of them off the hill. People vanished from sight, tumbling onto the roof of an adjacent building.

When we arrived at the central church, a man revealed a blue bucket and ladled clay-colored liquid into plastic cups. This was *chicha*, the corn-based beverage that the *Juego* was famous for serving. As Pedro explain it, *chicha* is not something you order at the corner bar. *Chicha* is a strong liquor and packed with calories. Throughout the three-day festival, participants drink *chicha* by the gallon, starting in the early morning and continuing until late at night. The drink makes them bold; they feel energized and impervious to the infernal heat. But *chicha* also makes them hopelessly drunk. Men staggered and crouched, overwhelmed by inebriation. Sometimes the man inside the bull costume simply fell over, and the others will help him up. Just watching them was exhausting.

"May I?" I asked the man with the bucket, and he poured *chicha* into my empty water bottle.

Lindsay took a swig, then Kylan, who handed the bottle to me. I gulped down liquid, which had the consistency of cider. But the taste surprised me; I had expected something dry and mealy, but the *chicha* smelled and tasted of wine.

"It's good," said Kylan, nodding.

"Yeah," I said.

I was relieved to hear this, because Kylan is picky about taste. I was also relieved to *say* it, because now I felt like I was participating. Sort of.

As the minutes crawled by, it dawned on me how rare this was: The *Juego* is not an entertainment. It is not performed for the sake of visitors. Nor is the *Juego* a sporting event, with points and referees. If anything, the *Juego* is like a full-contact church service, a symbolic ritual that represents the spirit of the people. Their stamina was impressive; they could continue to improvise skirmishes all day long. By early afternoon, many of the men wore Band-Aids and bandages. Forearms were scratched and some men were cross-eyed with drunkenness. But still they persisted, flinging themselves at the cloth animal, because that is what tradition demanded.

The shadows were lengthening when I turned a corner and saw them: A long procession of figures, dressed in togas made of leaves, their faces covered in demonic masks. Scores of people marched down the road, arms linked over shoulders, forming ranks of beastly warriors. Each mask was more elaborate than the last, each costume more impressive; eyes blazed, beaks jutted, noses flared, and real bird feathers blossomed around the wooden frame. Walking hip-to-hip, the leaf-covered men looked like walls of ivy advancing through the clouds of dust. Their numbers flowed through the village, arriving at last in a brown field. Hundreds of people surrounded the lawn, which had been roped off at the edges. Students and tourists had appeared for the first time that day, snapping pictures and staring in wonder. The tiny procession had accumulated hordes of Brunca and guests, because *this* was the festival's finale: a massive melee involving all the *diablitos* at once. Then the *diablitos* would stop, cover the bull with kindling, and set it on fire. The ritual was to end in a blaze of glory.

Throngs of warriors surrounded the bull as it whirled and feinted, attacked and collapsed. The *diablitos* swirled around and around, phalanxes of men linking arms. When the bull tackled them, some men went down in piles of limbs, hitting their heads on the ground. The setting sun bled through their silhouettes, the yellow haze subsumed them, and the *diablitos* looked more fearsome and defiant than ever. The Spanish had *not* been superstitious, after all; the masks were terrifying to behold, but also powerful, dignified. It was as if the vegetation itself had come alive, a sentient forest rearing against its trespassers. I would never see those masks the same way again. They weren't just art objects or funny costumes. The masks had purpose, here. They expressed the raging pride that human faces could not. They seemed, for the first time, alive.

The Working Poet

When I finally arrived at Veritas University to meet with the poet Luis Chaves, I felt a little giddy. I had read some of his work, yes, but I also knew his reputation. I knew that certain Tico friends would be jealous of our interview. They wouldn't believe that I got to sit down with Costa Rica's rising literary star. I've met my share of prominent writers over the years, but no one with Chaves' peculiar cachet.

Yet I also overestimated how long it would take to reach Veritas and arrived nearly two hours earlier than expected. After milling around the college's small campus, I decided to text Chaves. *Hi, it's Robert*, I wrote in Spanish. *I'm at Veritas, very early. Take your time, but I'm available when you're ready.*

He texted back almost immediately: *I'm on my way.*

The man who arrived in the campus' main court was nothing like I expected. In his press photos, Chaves has a bold presence—he wears fashionable glasses, his hair is densely curled, and his expression is both professorial and subversive. In one black-and-white portrait, he sits on a lotus position on a carpet of leaves, hands clasped, staring grimly at the photographer. But the Chaves who approached me was completely different: He's a compact 44-year-old with squinty eyes and whiffs of facial hair. He looked easygoing and good-humored; he seemed almost surprised to see me.

After shaking hands, he pointed to a campus snack bar. "Would you like something to drink?"

"Oh, I'm good, thank you."

He grabbed a bottle of iced tea and we sat down at a table. The sun had set and the evening was balmy. Students meandered through the court, some of them waiting for a film lecture to start. We probably didn't seem like a journalist and internationally acclaimed poet; we looked more like two adjunct professors passing time between classes.

"So," Chaves said, "what do you want to talk about?"

He sounded genuinely curious, as if he couldn't imagine why a reporter would call him up. This, I discovered, is the peculiar thing about Chaves: He is a prolific author, newspaper columnist, editor, and translator, and his work is reaching audiences around the world; yet his presence is gentle, almost shy. He has no agent, no publicist, no prepared speeches about his life and work. In person, he seems like a regular guy who works for a regular college. And in a way, his casual persona perfectly matches his writing.

Chaves is a most unlikely poet. Acquaintances describe him as a fairly ordinary child. His father was an amateur boxer, and Chaves was always a natural athlete. "Ever since I was a kid, I played sports," he recalled. Then he patted his stomach and added jovially, "Evidently not now. It's hard to find the time."

When he attended the University of Costa Rica, Chaves studied Agricultural Economics, or Agronomy. (The field is extremely popular in Costa Rica, where farming is still a major national industry.) Chaves was a serious young man. He worked an office job and always arrived on time. He seemed destined for a cubicle.

But then something happened, and no one could explain it to me, including Chaves. In short, Chaves became deeply interested in creative writing. To the surprise of many friends and relations, he abruptly turned away from agronomy—and the stable career everyone expected for him—and focused all his energy on writing. Chaves speaks excellent English, and he decided to work as a freelance translator. For 12 years, from 1999 to 2011, Chaves translated English text into Spanish for a diverse body of clients, including the World Wildlife Fund.

Meanwhile, Chaves participated in a writing workshop and developed his poetry. He used his natural discipline to develop his writing, and he traded work with fellow writers. He cultivated a friendship with César Maurel, a poet and visual artist originally from Paris.

"It was very informal," Maurel told me. "Chaves' writing is very narrative, very modern. It's more natural. There are many different themes."

In 1996, the press Editorial Guayacán published Chaves' first collection, *El Anónimo* (*The Anonymous*). Many poets may have felt satisfied, or even exhausted, after that first effort, but Ediciones Espiral published his second collection, *Los animales que imaginamos* (*The Animals We Imagine*) only a year later. This second book won the Sor Juana Inés de la Cruz Prize for Hispanic American Poetry. His 2001 book, *Historias Polaroid*, was shortlisted for a major Colombian literary award. By the time Editorial Germinal released his fourth book, *Chan Marshall*, in 2005, Chaves had established himself as a wellspring of superlative verse: *Chan Marshall* won the III Fray Luis de León Prize for Poetry.

Chaves might well have continued publishing poetry collections and winning awards. But one of the most significant chapters of his writing career happened in 2012, with the publication of *Asfalto*.

In *Asfalto*, a man and a woman take a road trip. They watch the highway through their windshield. They listen to The Kinks on their stereo. They stop at gas stations and motels. They sleep badly. In one ominous scene, Chaves describes the couple from the perspective of a surveillance camera. The chapters are short vignettes, but we soon realize that the couple's relationship is falling apart. The unnamed characters are doomed: "In the old wallet shaped by buttocks, a photograph of better times. The two of them in a park in another country. The photo in which she will forever gaze, not at him, who embraces her, but toward the unknown person who took it."

The full title is *Asfalto: un road poem*, and the book takes some cues from Jack Kerouac. But Chaves is also tougher, terser, and more biting than his beatnik predecessors. At exactly 100 pages, *Asfalto* packs a wallop. Some moments are lonely and bitter, others are grimly funny. On the page, *Asfalto* looks like prose; there are no stanzas, no line-breaks, no obvious rhyme or meter. But the book behaves like poetry. By the end, the reader is emotionally exhausted.

This eloquence is one reason Luis Chaves has become one of the most exciting living authors in Costa Rica. Chaves has broken down the borders between poet and prose writer. He has worked in many forms, and he seems committed to keep experimenting.

"I just like to write," Chaves said. "I don't care about the genre. It is up to the editors to decide where a book goes, but I give each one the same care."

Indeed, Chaves continues to depart more from traditional poetry with every new project. When Chaves started to contribute to the daily newspaper *La Nación*, he wrote largely about sports—his lifelong passion. The cultural intersection seemed strange: Poetry and athletics don't mix naturally. Yet Chaves feels they are the perfect marriage. "I've had this dilemma," he said. "I like the aesthetics of sports. I don't see a difference between a great poem and a great play in a soccer game." After a pause he added: "It's not about what you write about, but *how*."

I found it difficult to talk with people about Chaves, because no one felt qualified.

"I can't speak with you on the record," said an old acquaintance of Chaves. Her tone was low and tense, as if we were discussing state secrets. When I asked her why not, she explained that she was not an expert in poetry. Many others followed suit. The very idea of poetry intimidated them. During the week of National Poetry Day, celebrated on Jan. 31, readings were held in venues throughout San José, including various bars and the National Library. But people were reluctant to opine about Chaves.

"I just don't feel comfortable," said one poet. "It's hard to describe."

But Chaves holds a special place in this literary world. He has expanded the definition of what a writer can and should do. In recent years, he has authored the books *El Mundial 2010*, a nonfiction account of the 2010 World Cup, and *300 páginas*, a collection of columns and reportage. He has published broadly in literary journals and edited them as well. He continues to write regularly for *La Nación*. He even maintains his own blog, mysteriously called "Tetrabrik."

In a more pretentious country, I might expect Chaves to behave like an egomaniac. He has no exact equivalent elsewhere, but few U.S. or European authors are respected poets *and* popular sports commentators *and* write columns for one of the country's most respected newspapers. I have met creative writing students who essentially aspire to become Chaves. He is fairly young and accessible, yet his style is also challenging and even colloquial: In *Asfalto*, the characters say "*mae*" ("dude") in their dialogue, among other Tico idioms. Chaves is a major figure in Costa Rica's literary development, which is kind of like being a celebrity.

Throughout the hemisphere, Latin American countries each have their champion authors—poets and novelists who have won international acclaim and "represent" their nations. Gabriel García Márquez is the sage of Colombia. Octavio Paz is a literary heavyweight of Mexico. For bibliophiles, Peru is synonymous with Mario Vargas Llosa. Chile is nearly as well known for its fine literature as its wines: Jorge Luis Borges, Pablo Neruda, and the *enfant terrible* Roberto Bolaño all have posthumous oceans of fans.

Such authors have become staples of global literature classes. Many of them have won Nobel Prizes, among other honors. In the States, most college students can't earn their bachelor's degree without writing a paper on *One Hundred Years of Solitude*. Books by Paulo Coelho (Brazil) and Isabel Allende (Chile) are always runaway hits; their titles are routinely sold in airports and supermarkets, and in every major language. Some writers are more famous as personalities, like the rebellious Cuban poet Reinaldo Arenas and the politically charged Uruguayan writer Eduardo Galeano. A growing number of authors, like Junot Díaz and Sandra Cisneros, are de facto U.S. authors with powerful Latin American ties.

Costa Rica is different. Costa Rica has no literary superhero that foreigners would recognize. When tourists arrive at Juan Santamaría airport, they don't lug hefty novels about the Tico soul. They don't ask about Costa Rican poets or playwrights. There is no Costa Rican *Alchemist* or *Motorcycle Diaries* that inspired entire social movements in distant lands. And never mind the expats and tourists and foreign professors, who hardly count. There are plenty of Ticos who know little about Tico authors.

The irony is that Costa Rica has a very active literary scene, quiet though it appears. Foreigners would not realize this, because most of the writing exists only in Spanish, and even celebrated authors are unknown outside the country. Yet iconic figures still exist: Manuel González Zeledón (pen name "Magón") wrote stories at the turn of the century and founded the newspaper *El País*; today there is a Magón National Prize for Culture. There is a bust of novelist Yolanda Oreamuno outside the National Theater. Playwright Alberto Cañas Escalante was also a diplomat and lawyer, as well as Costa Rica's first minister of culture. One of Costa Rica's all-time greats, Carmen Naranjo, served as ambassador to Israel and has earned high praise all over the world. Daniel Garro Sánchez is a still-living science fiction writer, whose second novel, *La Máquina de los Sueños* (*The Dream Machine*), won the Carmen Lyra Youth Literature Contest. The prize is named after Carmen Lyra, who created "Tío Conejo," the Costa Rican equivalent of Br'er Rabbit. Tío Conejo is still so popular in Costa Rica that businesses and amusement parks use him as a mascot.

Before I moved to San José, I picked up a book called *Costa Rica: A Traveler's Literary Companion*. While the anthology was aimed at foreign tourists, it was something of a coup. Most of its stories had never before been translated into English (or any other language). For the first time, English-speaking readers could encounter essential Tico scribes. The stories cover the gamut of themes, such as farm life, marriage, lust, spirituality, and the land itself.

Yet most of the authors in *A Traveler's Literary Companion* are now old or deceased, and their works are somewhat historic. Today, Costa Rican writers still face the same crisis of world-be authors around the world: Why write books, much less plays or poetry, if nobody reads them? Creative youths can now study to produce TV shows and design videogames. They can build websites and lay out high-profile advertisements. Why trifle with something as antiquated as a novel?

More importantly, does it matter whether foreigners know and appreciate Costa Rican literature? And if it does, could Chaves be the voice that the world finally hears?

Yet Chaves doesn't show much interest in fame. When I asked him about the popularity of his work, whether he felt a certain responsibility as "one of the leading figures in Costa Rican poetry," Chaves was dismissive.

"I don't have any control over that," he said. "I don't think it's something you look for. It has nothing to do with what I'm doing."

Indeed, Chaves leads a fairly simple life. He is married with two young daughters. For the past two years, he has worked in marketing for Veritas' School of Film and Television. (When I receive press releases for the school's screenings and lectures, it is Chaves who sends them to me.) He teaches writing courses and continues to do translation work on the side. Many people at the university, including the security guards, seem to light up when asked about him; others have never heard his name in their lives.

"He works there?" one recent graduate told me. "Well, there's a high turnover rate at Veritas. People come and go."

When I asked Chaves about his writing process—a topic that can cause some writers to ramble for hours—he was nonchalant: "I'm not methodical or disciplined. There are times when I'm just reading, not writing. Sometimes I just write bits and pieces. Sometimes there are a few weeks when I write almost every day, an hour I can steal from work or family. I have a notebook. But in general I use it to jot down ideas and phrases that I can develop later on the computer."

In truth, Chaves is *not* a household name. As a rule, poets are the least-read creative writers, and even the most respected poets only attract niche followings. Chaves has no agent; few Costa Rican authors do. Most of his publishers are also friends and colleagues. Even tracking down his books can be a challenge: When I tried to find a copy of *Asfalto*, I visited Librería Internacional, one of Costa Rica's most popular chain bookstores. The clerk could only find one copy of one of his many books, and the volume took about four days to ship. (That said, it was heartening to know that a commercial bookstore actually stocked a local poet. One wonders whether Waldenbooks would have carried much Natasha Trethewey. Who is she, you ask? Oh, just the poet laureate of the United States.)

But neither can Chaves deny his impact on young Costa Rican readers and writers, who are inspired by his youthful, contemporary style. Unlike Yolanda Oreamuno and Carmen Naranjo, Chaves is still alive and well and composing books. He is not writing about the sleepy Costa Rica of yesteryear, but a modern nation of Shell stations and celebrity soccer players.

"Luis Chaves has become a watershed," said my friend David Monge, an aspiring poet who runs a popular writing workshop in Alajuela. "He touches everyday topics with plain language and poetic image. His works have influenced a new generation of writers, thus becoming a new paradigm of Costa Rican literature." Monge largely credits this success to an "explosion" of small presses, which have made publishing easier. "These publishers have come to give voice to a more underground and experimental literature—hence Chaves, with works that are outstanding, and at an international level."

Like Chaves himself, Monge feels there is a difference between being famous and reaching a broad readership.

"I question whether fame is important, because personally I think that the issue of disseminating the author's work is extremely important. Probably tomorrow, when a reader is looking at a Chaves book in a Madrid bookstore and is interested in the work of more Costa Rican authors, that will be good news for everyone."

At the moment, Chaves shows no signs of slowing down. He recently received a grant from the Ministry of Culture to write his first short story collection; again he plans to attempt a new genre for the first time. If the book is successful, Chaves could attract an even broader readership. His face recently graced the cover of *Buensalvaje*, a major Costa Rican literary review, accompanied by an unedited diary of 38 days of his life. Chaves has already published in such countries as Spain, Germany and Argentina, but it is hard to say whether he will reach a tipping point. Will his works be taught in universities, here and abroad? Might he stumble into the same maelstrom of fame as Bolaño and Márquez—men who skyrocketed from obscurity to global eminence almost overnight? Only time will tell.

For me, the most pressing question is this: Does Chaves expect his work to be translated into English? Will Chaves, a professional translator himself, one day see his books recast in his second language? Will *Asfalto*, perhaps retitled *Asphalt*, affect a new generation of English-speaking readers as well? To date, not one of his books has ever been translated in its entirety. Has this possibility ever occurred to him?

"I am convinced that Chaves would lose nothing when translated into English," said César Maurel, who has been reading the poet's work for years. "There are already some translations and the magic is still there. Of course there are many 'Tico' elements, but I think his talent will not be lost if he establishes a relationship with a good translator."

During our conversation in the quad, I save this question for last, because I'm selfishly fascinated by that possibility. I imagine how many of my monolingual Gringo friends are missing out.

"Would you consider English editions of your books?" I ask eagerly. "Do you think your work would make sense in English?"

"Well," says Chaves, shrugging. "That depends on whether someone is interested in translating it."

Saving Hearts

Like thousands of expats before her, María Fejervary first came to Costa Rica on vacation. She came with her kids and another family. They spent some time on the beach. They enjoyed the sunny weather. They ate the food and wandered around, like any other tourist.

But Fejervary also spotted prostitutes. On the central Pacific coast, Fejervary was appalled to see sex workers standing in the streets, in full view. She noticed how young many of them seemed. While adult prostitution is legal in Costa Rica, Fejervary guessed that many were actually underage, coerced into the trade by abusive criminals.

"We were looking for a fun place to vacation," she would later tell me. "We had no idea about any sex tourism here."

When Fejervary returned to California, the images stuck with her. She knew a little about sex slavery and human trafficking, but now she decided to stock up on books, articles, official reports. She read everything she could get her hands on, and she started going to conferences. Fejervary wanted to help the victims in a meaningful way.

"When I went back to the States, I felt very called to come and do something," she said. "Nobody's really doing anything to fight it. There's so much change that needs to happen in this country. It's not about pointing fingers, it's about changing things."

Slowly, Fejervary formulated a mission: She would return to Costa Rica. She would build a rehabilitation center for young survivors of sex slavery. She would create an official nongovernmental organization, certified by the government-run Child Welfare Office (PANI). She would house, feed, educate and provide therapy for as many kids as possible.

Fejervary was no expert in human trafficking. She was not yet fluent in Spanish, despite having lived a short time in Mexico, and she didn't have a college degree. She knew little about Costa Rican bureaucracy. Fejervary had spent most of her adult life running a daycare center and volunteering at homeless shelters. What did she know about founding a facility in another country?

Yet today, Fejervary is founder and president of Salvando Corazones ("Saving Hearts"). After an uphill battle that has lasted nearly half a decade, she has met every one of her goals. And if she can steer the organization steadily, she may help save a generation of girls from lifelong abuse.

When I met with Fejervary in 2014, it was Costa Rica's Independence Day, and the town of Tilarán was frenetic with activity. Fejervary had brought her colleagues and young wards to see the parades, and downtown Tilarán was flooded with marching bands. The occasion was a fitting one for her outing: Costa Rica's Día de la Independencia focuses a lot of attention on children. At night, kids pour into parks and avenues with homemade lamps, or *faroles*, for the Lantern Parade, and the next morning young musicians play instruments and whirl batons.

"Aren't they cute?" said Fejervary as a garrison of preteen brass players marched down the main street. She looked happy and relaxed; she wasn't the fiery activist I had expected. Then she proposed to sit down at a local *soda* and chat. We broke away from the group, found a table, and ordered a couple of Coca-Colas.

"There are very few women out there who *choose* prostitution," began Fejervary. "If somebody comes into a brothel and he knows the doorman, then nobody cares what happens in there. These customers need to go to jail. If we don't hold people accountable, they're not going to change their ways. We have to teach our children, at the kindergarten level, how to treat women. We have to create a society where exploitation is *not* okay."

Fejervary is a straight talker. At 54 years old, she has a rugged smile and moves slowly, owing to many painful surgeries, including a recent operation on her back. In conversation, she is unpretentious and seems to hold nothing back. She has strong opinions about certain Costa Rican ministries, about the justice system, about well-known individuals she has met, and she expresses these opinions freely. Only one thing seems to matter to her: the recovery of the girls in her care.

"Why are you interested in this?" she asked me abruptly.

It was a good question. I explained my longtime interest in the issue of human trafficking, especially sex slavery. Compared to war or gang violence, the subject earns only a fraction of the media attention. The problem is pandemic and has ruined innumerable lives, yet unlike other social problems, people don't like to talk about sex slavery. The subject seems too intimate, too painful and horrifying, to debate openly. Polite society will gab about drug addiction and serial killers all day long, but the thought of forcing a 12-year-old to have sex for money is too awful to contemplate.

On a more personal level, I told Fejervary that I had been solicited by scores of sex workers around the world, almost always in the street. All of them were adults, as far as I could tell. But it is difficult for a casual observer to distinguish consensual sex workers from women forced into the trade. I find this particularly unsettling, because millions of johns are exactly like me: normal-looking male professionals from a developed country. My interactions have always been brief—I would never hire a sex worker—but I have always wondered what happens to these people. (I say people, rather than women, because many of them are men or transgendered.) For sex workers lucky enough to escape the racket, how do they acclimate to normal life?

Satisfied with my response, Fejervary said, "Let's go visit the home." And we headed for our cars.

Initially, Fejervary had to decide where to start her program—that is, which country. While it was Costa Rica that had motivated her to take action, she considered a variety of possible nations.

"I had two prerequisites," recalled Fejervary. "I had to like the weather, and I had to be able to learn the language. So that ruled out Asia." She laughed. After a few years of immersion, she now speaks Spanish very well.

Fejervary had visited this country on vacation more than once, and she finally whittled down her options and decided that Costa Rica was the most fitting base of operations. Fejervary founded Salvando Corazones as a nonprofit in 2010, but that was only the beginning of a difficult slog. Costa Rica already had a similar recovery program called the Rahab Foundation, which had earned praise for helping former sex workers. But Rahab works primarily with adults, and clients do not live on the premises. Fejervary wanted to improve upon its model: work entirely with children, and give them shelter as well.

To begin her search, Fejervary visited the Lake Arenal area with vague plans to obtain a property. She wanted to base her facility in a rural setting, far from sex trafficking hubs like San José and the province of Puntarenas. She had concerns that children might try to seek out former caretakers, no matter how abusive, because the kids yearned for familiarity. Many of the children would inevitably have substance abuse problems, and she had to curb access to drug dealers.

I asked her how she picked this place in particular.

"*It* picked *me*," said Fejervary with a knowing chuckle.

During her visit, she said, Fejervary decided to sit down outside and take a breather. As she did so, a random man approached her and asked whether she was looking for real estate. The man wasn't a licensed agent, but he guided her around the region, suggesting different sellers and properties. When she found the building that would one day become Salvando Corazones, she was awestruck: The large structure stood on a grassy bluff overlooking Lake Arenal. The surrounding lot had plenty of room for a garden and some livestock.

"I stood there and thought: 'This is it,'" remembered Fejervary.

The building had some problems. It was new, but also unfinished. The former owner had foreclosed, which meant Fejervary would have to spearhead final construction of the interior. Meanwhile, there was a family of squatters living inside – as well as their two cows.

Fejervary is no stranger to difficult, hands-on tasks: A native of Palo Alto, California, she has encountered plenty of challenges during her time working in homeless shelters, as well as running a daycare for 28 years. Fejervary is open about her own history of sexual abuse—she says that her teachers took advantage of her when she was young—and she uses this experience to work with vulnerable people.

"I tell the kids, 'You can heal from it, and it doesn't have to define you,'" said Fejervary. "'But it *is* a part of you.'"

Fejervary has four adult children, two biological and two adopted. When she said that she had adopted two of her children from Russia, I was startled. Russian orphanages are perhaps the most disreputable in the world, where poor facilities, brutal caretakers, and rampant abuse are routinely reported. When she arrived in Russia to finalize the adoption process, she found herself counting $100 bills in a secluded room in front of dubious men.

"I thought to myself, 'I'm involved in human trafficking,'" she recalled.

In short, Fejervary had faced tough personalities and tangled bureaucracy many times before, and she was determined to succeed. She managed to have her organization certified through PANI, enabling her to legally care for young victims of sex slavery. The certification was specific: Fejervary can only receive children and teenagers assigned to her by PANI. All of the children are female, and none of them can be pregnant. If a girl is discovered to be pregnant, Salvando Corazones must forfeit her to PANI.

During my visit, Fejervary said hello to several locals in Tilarán, exchanging waves and smiles. I asked her how she had adapted to living there, whether she had made any friends.

"They all know me," she said grudgingly.

On top of all the other challenges, Fejervary claimed the community was suspicious of her intentions. She said they called her a child molester behind her back. In the year since the Corazones facility opened, she has had to fight the tide of gossip. Only recently has she sensed a change for the better.

The Corazones facility is secluded and hard to find, which is a good thing. But I wondered whether a relatively nearby town like Tilarán might also have its share of sex workers.

Fejervary shrugged. "I'm sure it does," she said. "But it's everywhere."

"Everywhere" is no exaggeration: In the United States, the Federal Bureau of Investigations estimates that 293,000 minors are currently "at risk of becoming victims of commercial sexual exploitation." On the international stage, an estimated two million children are exploited each year in the global commercial sex trade, according to activist group Equality Now. There are well-known hotspots, like Bangkok, Thailand, and Goa, India, but the geography of underage sex trafficking is borderless.

Costa Rica is one of those hotspots. For sex tourists, the nation is a favored destination, where transport and trysts are easy to arrange, and many forms of prostitution are legal. For watchdogs, the nation is notorious for its sexual exploitation. In its 2014 report on human trafficking, the U.S. State Department identified Costa Rica as a "Tier 2" Watch List nation. "The Government of Costa Rica does not fully comply with the minimum standards for the elimination of trafficking," noted the report. "However, it is making significant efforts to do so. In 2013, authorities convicted an increased number of trafficking offenders compared to the previous year and created a dedicated prosecutorial unit for human trafficking and smuggling."

"I don't trust statistics," said Fejervary several times during my visit. She has a point. Sex crimes and human trafficking are both routinely underreported, no matter where they take place, and it is impossible to get a precise picture of the situation in Costa Rica. But the problem is glaring: The same week I visited Salvando Corazones, Costa Rican police raided a suspected prostitution ring in San José, arresting six suspects. Police claimed to have rescued 70 "sex slaves" from Nicaragua, Costa Rica, and the Dominican Republic.

The sex trade in this country is infamous around the world. In 2007, the writer Sean Flynn wrote a vivid account of Costa Rica's sex industry for *GQ*. Little has changed since Flynn's story; his unflinching descriptions could as easily be written today. Flynn was writing about the legal sex trade for an upscale men's magazine, but his conclusion was damning. After describing airport posters that warn against child prostitution, Flynn writes, "Welcome to Costa Rica, where it is illegal to rape children. Where it is necessary, in fact, to remind every single tourist entering the country that it is wrong to rape children."

When discussing the sex trade and sexual exploitation, the distinction is important: While many critics passionately object to any kind of prostitution, prostitution by adults is legal in Costa Rica. Pimping, child prostitution, rape, sexual slavery, or smuggling foreigners across the border for the express purpose of selling their bodies are illegal. In theory, these crimes are a separate issue from the legal adult sex trade.

In practice, it's not so simple. Prostitution is legal and regulated in all kinds of unexpected places, like Switzerland and Turkey. Yet in a country like Costa Rica where the industry is lucrative, the GDP is low, and laws are haphazardly enforced, a thriving legal sex trade arguably opens the door to illegal activity, including the sexual abuse of children. Costa Rica already hosts a steady stream of sex tourists, and many of them are predatory. Self-made pimps can find children, imprison them, and force them to service clients. The underground industry wreaks unspeakable damage on minors, and the nation is almost completely unprepared to rehabilitate the victims.

As the U.S. State Department's report put it: "Victim services remained inadequate… Government capacity to proactively identify and assist victims, particularly outside of the capital, remained weak."

For full rehabilitation, Fejervary says a child needs at least two years of in-house care and intensive therapy. Survivors of Costa Rica's sex trade likely number in the thousands. Since the facility started operating about a year ago, Salvando Corazones has cared for a total of 18 children. The oldest just turned 15.

Each morning at Salvando Corazones, the girls wake up in bunks, make their beds, and get dressed. From 6:50 to 7:15 a.m., they eat breakfast together in the open-plan living room, where the windows are broad and offer a breathtaking view of the valley and lake. They start class at 7:30 a.m. Lunch lasts from noon to 12:30. They have two 15-minute snack breaks. From 4:30 to 5:30 p.m., they get together for group therapy.

"Every hour is regimented," said Fejervary as she guided me through the house. "Their home lives usually didn't have any structure. They're *looking* for structure."

The rigid curriculum is based on years of group-home research in the United States, but Fejervary and her staff have worked hard to embellish that rubric: The facility has a library with several hundred books, a Foosball table, a table tennis set, and board games. Nearly every bed and couch has its own stuffed animal, which the kids constantly pick up and embrace. The girls earn points for good behavior, but they can also lose privileges (mostly TV) for bad behavior.

What's an example of bad behavior?

"Using bad words," said Fejervary. But even in that case, the "bad" vocabulary is established as a group. The girls collectively decide what language is offensive to them. This is particularly significant in Spanish, where "*puta*" ("whore") is considered one of the most vulgar insults, and many other slurs are disparaging of sexuality and women in particular.

Fejervary led me outside, where the hill sloped downward, toward a wooded defile, where an unseen creek flowed past the property. The shell of a building stood next door, its interior half-finished and full of building materials. Fejervary said that this building would eventually serve as a schoolhouse, but Salvando Corazones still required as much as $20,000 to finish construction.

"I don't understand why it's so hard to get finances," said Fejervary.

Indeed, the facility's operating costs amount to $31,000 per month, including food, utilities, wages for the full-time psychologist and teacher, and innumerable other expenses. Fejervary says that PANI is supposed to provide financial support, but so far the institution has only sent her kids. She has gotten this far thanks in large part to donations from a variety of sources.

If Fejervary can secure the funds she needs and Salvando Corazones becomes stable and sustainable, she wants to create an offshoot facility for pregnant girls, and then a third facility for boys, who are among the least-reported victims of sexual abuse. But for now they will have to wait until the schoolhouse is finished, among many smaller tasks.

We hiked down the hill, toward a coop with several chickens. The birds provide fresh eggs, and the girls use the surrounding gardens to cultivate carrots, onions, cucumber, squash, and herbs. Many of the young residents encounter a completely new diet when they arrive: Because vegetables are expensive, they often subsisted exclusively on rice and beans until they entered the PANI system. The Salvando Corazones staff ensures that they eat well-rounded meals, particularly veggies.

Back at the house, Fejervary pointed out the many murals that decorated the walls. Nearly every surface has its own colorful painting, such as rainbows and animals. In the stairwell, silhouettes of girls blowing dandelion seeds adorn the surfaces; this nook was called "the wishing wall."

A noticeable omission is the heavy religious symbolism present in some rehabilitation facilities. There are no giant crucifixes on the walls, no inspirational Christian posters, no Bibles lying around the furniture. Fejervary herself grew up in a nonreligious household, and it was only when her young son, many years ago, took an interest in the local Presbyterian church that Fejervary attended a service. Now her son is pursuing a Ph.D. in Old Testament studies.

"I'm in the middle," said Fejervary. "I like church and I like prayer, but I don't need to call myself a Christian or anything else. I don't need a title for that."

As bucolic as the residence is, life at Salvando Corazones is rife with challenges. Girls have attempted to run away. Self-harm is a constant concern. Residents often have to learn basic domestic skills, like regular bathing, tidying up, or using toiletries. Breakdowns are common. During my visit, one of the girls burst into tears and sobbed for nearly an hour. At such moments, the girls are encouraged to visit Lorna Bastos, the in-house psychologist, in her private office. Because of their protracted trauma, anything could trigger a panic attack or emotional outburst, and the staff has to be prepared at any moment. Bastos provides one-on-one counseling. Such constant emotional problems might be wearying, but Bastos maintains a good attitude.

"Work problems I can leave at work," said Bastos. "I'm thankful that God gave me the ability to separate personal problems from work problems or the problems of others. Many years ago, when I was a student, a psychology professor told me that a person's brain should be like a stereo that can play several CDs. Every time I work, I put in the work CD, and when I leave, I take it out and put in my personal life CD, so that I don't mix these CDs in my mind."

"Would you like to talk with them?" Fejervary finally asked.

Although the girls themselves were the most important part of Salvando Corazones, I was shy about actually speaking with them. For obvious reasons, I couldn't name them or photograph their faces, but I was surprised that Fejervary had invited me to the residence at all. Having grown up in a household where patient privacy issues were a big deal—my mother is a psychologist—I am fanatical about that issue, and I knew that the nearby La Fortuna Orphanage dissuades journalists from even contacting residents, much less visiting.

But I was happy to talk with two of the residents, whom I will call Zania and Alegría. Zania was bookish and bespectacled, and she said her favorite subject was math. She had lived at Salvando Corazones for 14 months, where she loved to study English, arithmetic and cake decorating.

"I like yoga," she said, nodding. "I'm getting more flexible."

Zania was particularly fond of the equine therapy program. When a local organization, Vínculo con Caballo, contacted Salvando Corazones and offered free therapy sessions with their horses, Fejervary was skeptical. "I thought, 'Girls have fun with horses, that'll be fun to do.' I had no concept of what it was. And I certainly did not believe that it was possible to get the kind of results we're getting from it." During the group's first visit, the children were blindfolded and put in the same space as the horses, and each horse then gravitated toward one of the girls. Then they mounted the saddles and were led through an obstacle course.

"It's really fun," said Zania. "The horse chooses me, and I choose him. I was afraid at first, but now I'm not."

Alegría had spent seven months at Salvando Corazones, where she also loved math and reading. "I get to think," she said. Before, when she looked out the window, she saw only ugly things. "Lots of problems, pollution, injustice. Now I see the lake, the volcano, the light, lots of trees, nature."

Perhaps the most astonishing thing about Zania and Alegría was how normal they seemed. Spotted on a street or in a schoolyard, they would strike me as happy, giggly teenagers, perfectly well-adjusted, as innocent and fun-loving as neighborhood Girl Scouts. It is a testament to how much Salvando Corazones has accomplished: Many residents arrived with second-grade educations, and within one year they are testing into high-school level classes. Fejervary suggests that Salvando Corazones' instruction is better than in most public schools.

What does Alegría want to be when she grows up?

"I wanted to be a gynecologist," she said. "But first I want to be a schoolteacher, then earn a master's in math, then become a lawyer, then an agricultural engineer…" She paused and smiled brightly. "Because I want to do everything."

Whatever happens to Salvando Corazones, whatever challenges lie ahead, Fejervary looked as embedded as she could be. She had given up a satisfying job in a place that she loved. Her children are spread out now, and she could just as easily spend her time visiting them. But Fejervary has work to do, and if her budget will allow her, the organization will expand, providing some of the most desperately needed resources in the country right now.

"The kids always ask me, 'Would you die for us?'" said Fejervary. "And I say, 'Absolutely.' Then they ask, 'How come my mother didn't love me the way you love me?' I say, 'She wasn't capable. But you deserve it. You just have to love yourself enough to accept it.'"

Unas Aventuras

Wiping Out

"Get ready," shouted Dante as water swooshed around us. "Okay, here it comes! Get on the board, Robert! *Now!*"

I jumped upward and threw my body on the surfboard. My stomach smacked hard and my hands clasped the sides in a talon grip. I pried my eyes upward, toward the beach, because I knew that's what I was supposed to do, but the urge to look down at the scratched fiberglass, or to look behind at the oncoming wave, was almost unbearable.

"*Reeeady?*" Dante said tensely.

The lukewarm water slipped beneath me like a rug being drawn back. I could sense its movement as I had never sensed it before, though I didn't yet understand the shift in the water's skin. Then, just as a long hiss announced the unseen wave, Dante shouted, "*Go, Robert! Paddle! Paddle! Paddle!*"

My arms smashed into the water, a cartoonish crawl-stroke, and I inched the board forward as the water's surface warped and curved.

"*Now, Robert!*" shrieked Dante, his voice muted by the gathering roar. "*Stand up!*"

I pushed myself up, slid my feet along the board, then angled my heels. I felt my back instinctively arch, my arms elongate into the position of an archer. My posture mimicked every surf movie I had ever seen, but effortlessly, as if my body had waited 35 years for this moment to pose. I was standing so high that I felt vertigo, and the wave pushed me along, a velvety glide toward the shore. For an instant, I remembered what it was like to balance on a bicycle for the first time—the same breeze, the same smooth propulsion. My throat struggled to emit a triumphant laugh, but it seized.

The wave dissipated, the board slowed, and then I stepped off, tumbling into the froth. The board drifted away, tugging at the leash attached to my ankle. Now I could laugh, fully and from the diaphragm. A cackle drowned in the ocean's noise.

I stood up, I marveled. *I stood up on the first try!*

Surfing has always been exotic to me. Having lived most of my life in cold, landlocked places, the absence of oceanfront and warm weather made surfing seem like an impossible fantasy. Until I spent time in Costa Rica, I had never really seen surfers in person. When I saw surfers, they were on TV, flipping off crests and speeding through "tubes" with ease. Aside from furrowed brows, pro surfers betray no anxiety that cubic tons of water are curling around their fragile bodies, threatening to crush them. I couldn't even imagine it.

The first time I visited Jacó, on the central Pacific coast, I saw surfers on the bay. Some were skilled, skidding along the breaks and hurling themselves into the air, but most of them were not. They stood up, they fell down. They perched on their boards and let the waves roll under them. They bobbed in groups and chatted. Most had regular body types, and some were even flabby.

The waves in Jacó are gentle and long, not the 20-footers I had always seen in calendars. It dawned on me that most surfers are casual amateurs, just as most basketball players play pickup games on neighborhood blacktops. I spotted a hairy, middle-aged guy venturing into the waves as he dragged a longboard behind him. *If that guy can do it,* I thought, *I can do it.*

Then I had my chance: My friend Andrés had business in Jacó, and we decided to make a weekend trip. Andrés said he could schedule a free two-hour class for Kylan and me, thanks to an arrangement he had with a local hotel.

"We're gonna be surfers!" we exclaimed to each other periodically as the day approached.

We were elated, because an unthinkable dream would soon come true. We liked the simplicity of surfing—boards are affordable, and daily rentals are downright cheap. Gear is simple, and a single rash guard can last for years. There is no need for cleats, pads, helmets, or sticks. There is no engine to maintain, no fuel to buy, no special gloves or shoes to replace. The arena is free and as big as the ocean. A surfer requires no judge or spotters or ball boys or caddies. Barring the threat of riptides, a surfer can throw on a swimsuit, grab a board, and spend hours alone in the water.

Surfing also has its own culture, which comes with rituals and vocabulary, and although I never imagined saying phrases like "Eddie would go" and "Mad backhand, bro," I liked the idea of chilling at cabanas with longhaired friends and bragging about the day's exploits. Serious surfers carry with them a mystical optimism that I've always enjoyed.

Of course, Costa Rica is also the perfect place to learn how to surf. The beaches are packed with toned young wave-riders, and they come here from all over the world. Costa Rica earned global fame in 1966 with the release of *The Endless Summer*, a surf documentary of biblical renown, which featured the country prominently. All over the world, surfers ache to visit places like Puerto Viejo and Malpaís. And here we were, a reasonable drive from either coast.

But we also had no idea how we would fare. Kylan and I both love solo sports, and we are both skilled alpine skiers, yet this felt completely different. Most sports have static environments, like a field or court. Most outdoor activities have predictable courses that change only slowly; runners and rock climbers can see oncoming storms, snowboarders can anticipate an icy day. In contrast, surfing changes every second. Each wave is distinct from all others. The height and power and arc of a single wave will never be repeated, and there are always exceptions to the pattern. The one thing most athletes can trust—the ground beneath their feet—is the surfer's greatest adversary.

We took our first lesson with Dante, a petite-yet-muscular instructor from Venezuela. A rising sun bathed the beach in rosy light. Dante unloaded the surfboards from his truck, asked a few questions, and cut to the chase.

"I'm not going to teach you a lot of tricks and techniques that you're just going to forget anyway," he said. "Today we are just going to learn how to stand up on the board."

In preparation for our first lesson, Kylan and I had watched a few YouTube tutorials about the "pop-up"—the act of lifting oneself into a standing position. Since most video footage of pro surfers takes place in mid-glissade, I had never really noticed the first stage of the process. Dante demonstrated how to lie on the board, where to put our bodies, and how to hold the sides. The pop-up was a lot like a push-up, and the movement felt graceful.

Dante refined our positioning with each attempt.

"Robert, remember to angle your feet," he advised. "Keep them closer together, or you won't be able to keep your balance."

The practice rounds felt silly, since they took place on the dry sand, but we knew that there was no better way to do it. We stood up over and over, spreading our arms as we had seen in a hundred beach movies.

When Dante was satisfied with our progress, he guided us toward the water. We lugged our longboards, which were larger and heavier than we'd expected. Where downhill skiers graduate to longer and longer skis, surfers do the opposite—with increased skill, the board itself generally shrinks. Pro surfers sacrifice the stability of a longboard for the dexterity of a shortboard. As we tromped through the lukewarm water, the longboard felt gigantic, like a polyurethane raft wedged under my armpit.

We waded to our chests, and Dante gave us our final instructions. He held my board and signaled when I should crawl atop it. He watched the horizon for swells, but I had no idea what he was looking for. This was part of the art of surfing – knowing which waves would crescendo just the right way and launch the board forward.

After my first successful pop-up, I looked back and saw Kylan lift herself to her feet. Like me, she only sustained herself for a few seconds before tumbling into the foam, but I shouted toward her, "*Awesome! That was awesome!*" It's always exciting to succeed at something new and unfamiliar, but surfing was something else. We doggy-paddled back into the water, and Dante prepped a few more runs. Our pop-ups improved with every attempt, and when we finally toddled to shore, we felt victorious.

"We're totally going to be surfers," Kylan proclaimed at lunch. Our destiny seemed clear.

For weeks we boasted of our astonishing new skill. We bragged to our parents over Skype. We compared anecdotes with friends who had also taken one complete surfing class. We catalogued longboard prices and considered buying a roof rack for our car. We imagined our new life as itinerant beach bums, working remotely for half the day and waiting for a local stoner to call through our bungalow window, "Surf's up, *mae!*"

After long delays, we scheduled a second class with a different instructor, Rico. He had us demonstrate our pop-ups on the beach.

"Huh," he said, nodding approvingly. "You look like you know what you're doing."

Kylan and I traded knowing smiles. *Of course we know what we're doing. We're freaking prodigies.*

Showing off for our new instructor was our downfall. Rico escorted us into heavier breaks, and he taught us how to roll onto our backs, hugging our boards, so that the waves could slosh over us. Dante had (wisely) not covered this step, and we burned so much energy fighting through the current that we were soon exhausted. Rico had us straddle our boards and float for a few minutes, then he told us to get into position.

We hadn't realized how much effort Dante's grip had saved us. Now that we were fending for ourselves, the waves felt anarchic. Kylan has never been a strong swimmer, and my upper body has atrophied since my adolescent swim classes.

After 20 minutes of watching us flail, Rico ushered us toward a calmer stretch of water. He looked disappointed. We were not the budding surf champs he had expected, just a couple of rookies who knew how to stand up on a level surface. Rico did exactly as Dante had done, holding our boards and signaling when to paddle. We had regressed. We were back to training wheels. Rico looked increasingly bored as he gave us banal suggestions: "Okay, maybe bend your knees a little more. Keep your feet closer together. Try standing more in the middle…"

An hour later, we could barely lug our boards to the waiting truck. Our arms dangled, our jaws were slack, and we yearned to collapse in the sand. We had finished our first class in triumph, but now we had tasted *real* surfing, and the waves had wrecked us. Perhaps we had no future after all.

A few days later, I stumbled into a collection of quotes by famous pro surfers. Many were funny. ("I surf to get tan," said Shane Dorian). Others were startlingly profound. ("We're all equal before a wave," Laird Hamilton). Hamilton also said, "Wiping out is an underappreciated skill." I cherished his modesty, considering that Hamilton is among the most famous surfers of all time, and he has routinely surfed 11-meter swells—roughly the height of a three-story building.

But it was Phil Edward, surfing pioneer and co-star of *The Endless Summer*, who impressed me most: "The best surfer out there is the one having the most fun."

Despite our ruinous second attempt, we *had* had fun. And we would again. Come hell or uncomfortably high water, we would try surfing a third time, and maybe one day, we'd get to try the shortboard.

Oral History

There was a moment, just after the sheet was drawn over my head, when I thought, *Maybe I shouldn't do this.*

The sheet covered my eyes. It had an opening just large enough to expose my numbed mouth. I felt like a heretic at the hands of the Spanish Inquisition.

What are three rotten teeth? I thought. *Couldn't I do this another time—like in 10 years? Is all this really necessary?*

But the Novocain had already been injected. The assistant had punctured me a dozen times, including three excruciating shots to the hard palette. I had already swallowed a pair of unidentified pills. They had already asked what kind of music I liked, and now the Beatles were playing from a nearby desktop computer. A huge fraction of my bank account was wadded in my pocket. I had made the decision to have my teeth pulled in Costa Rica, and now it was time.

"Hello, Robert," said Dr. Anglada as his silhouette loomed through the fabric.

I tried to say "*hola*," but because of the numbness it came out "oh-ah."

"You are doing well today?" Dr. Anglada said. I could hear the tinkle of tools, the squeak of a chair.

"Ey-hoy dee-an," I said. *Estoy bien.*

I wondered whether the anesthetic would suffice, not because I doubted Dr. Anglada's abilities, but because I imagined some anomaly in my nervous system. *Maybe I have hypersensitive nerves. Should I ask for more? Maybe they should have knocked me out. But aren't there all those horror stories about people staying awake through their surgery? Why the hell did I agree to do this?*

"Now, Robert," said the surgeon in a soothing baritone, "I am going to cut the tooth in half, so it is easier to extract. Are you ready?"

I heard myself slur the word "*Sí*."

And then I hear the whir of a tiny electric saw.

Ever since I lost my last baby tooth, my teeth have been a lifelong nightmare. They grew at freakish angles, which led to years of braces, plus the full orthodontic arsenal: rubber bands, a bite plane, special toothbrushes, the works. When the braces finally came off, I lost my retainer for six weeks and the teeth shifted back into place. A year later, I had my wisdom teeth removed, and after the surgery I suffered head-splitting migraines for a solid month.

Despite these misadventures, I've only needed one filling. Dentists are usually impressed by my hygiene, although they vociferously wish I would floss more. So imagine my surprise, in 2004, when my right molar suddenly *broke*. I was sitting in a computer lab in Pittsburgh, and when I bit down during an especially pensive moment, the tooth just collapsed. My tongue turned up a chunk of off-white bone. For years, I had dreamed of my teeth falling out—a common nightmare, usually linked to anxiety—but now it had actually happened.

The deterioration continued, first in the right molar, then the left, until each tooth was a kind of stub. No one could see these jagged, blackened remains, so I never gave them much thought. But the molars were tethered to an even worse problem: Because my upper wisdom teeth hadn't been removed, they sometimes impacted the other teeth. Every six months or so, my wisdom teeth would shift, reminding me that they existed, and the pain was excruciating. For a full week, twice a year, I could barely eat an orange slice.

"Please," Kylan coaxed, "can you just go see a dentist?"

I don't like dentists, of course, but that wasn't the issue. Rather, I was a freelance writer and had no insurance. For 10 years, the American healthcare system was a completely foreign concept to me; I didn't even know that dental coverage existed. Twenty-somethings don't waste their money on oral surgery when they only make $15,000 a year.

When I finally *did* see a dentist, I could only afford it because of a Groupon deal that Kylan found online. I found the office in Pittsburgh's South Side, and the place was wood-paneled and dark. The sign above the front door was a wooden tooth, weather beaten and barely legible. The dentist wordlessly cleaned my teeth until he reached the dead molars. When he saw them, the dentist sat back, stared at the ceiling, and angrily sighed.

"Why do people do this?" he seethed.

"Ooh aht?" I said. *Do what?*

"Why didn't you have these removed yet?" He sounded accusatory, as if I had insulted him with my poverty.

Soon after, a premolar collapsed as well, causing me to panic. The tooth was much more visible than the molars, and now I felt pain. I could only chew on the other side of my mouth. Every time I ate, I looked like Popeye.

When I finally received dental coverage through my wife's insurance, I visited a significantly better dentist. The assistants were professional and kind—right up until the head dentist arrived. When she flew into the room, the dentist looked hurried and annoyed. She ripped open my mouth, gave my teeth a cursory examination, and said: "Those have to come out." She looked at the premolar and shook her head in disgust. "That one's abscessed. It'll have to come out, too."

"Okay," I said. "How much will that cost?"

"Well, it'll probably take the rest of your insurance," she said, snapping off her gloves.

"Can I replace the one? I'd rather not have—you know—a *gap*."

She closed her eyes. She looked furious, at wit's end. What kind of egotist was I? What was wrong with a visibly missing tooth? There were plenty of salt-miners and serial killers who had missing teeth. What made me so revoltingly vain?

"If you want an implant," she said slowly, "you can't do it here."

"Okay," I said, waiting for a follow up. When she said nothing, I added: "So, where then?"

"The University of Pittsburgh," she said. "They can put in the titanium screw, but you'll have to wait four months for it to graft to the bone. I can add the implant here."

This was the first time anyone had suggested fusing anything to my skeletal structure, and the only thing worse than an obviously missing tooth was a spike jutting out of my gums. So I gave up on that idea. I could keep my rotting, pain-inducing tooth, because there was obviously no alternative.

When it came to dentistry, the American healthcare system had done a grand total of nothing for me. More than 20 years after my teeth grew in, they were still a crowded, unsightly mess, and every six months I had to subsist on soup and ice cream, because the pain was so unbearable.

Then we moved to Costa Rica, and dentists were everywhere. Our first apartment was surrounded by dentists' offices. Expats gushed about the affordable cleanings and surgery. "When you see an expat," said our U.S. friend Harry, "ask how his teeth are doing. Some people come to Costa Rica just to get a cleaning."

We found Dr. Anglada's practice online. We wanted an English-speaking surgeon, and we wanted someone with a good reputation. During our first phone call, the surgeon's assistant, Bill, cheerfully talked with me for 25 minutes. He had lived in the United States for many years and spoke perfect American English.

"So you're looking for three extractions and an implant," Bill summarized. "We can do that. You can come in and we'll give you an estimate. When are you available?"

The truth is, I *still* might have waffled for another decade. I was so weary of failed dental work, lofty expenses, and condescending hygienists that the thought of having my teeth pulled out made me glum. The real hero of this saga is Kylan, who coerced me for years to get my mouth fixed. Each time I felt a wave of pain, she begged me to prioritize. "This is your *body*," she said. "I'm not going to like you with dentures."

So I went. The office was bright, spotless, and intimate. I filled out some forms and waited only a few minutes. When I asked to use their WiFi signal, the receptionist smiled and said, "Of course." They took me into a backroom, where a nervous young man took my X-rays. But instead of a single general X-ray, he took a dozen different close-ups. This ended up costing me nothing extra.

The surgeon arrived, and I was blindsided by his appearance: Dr. Anglada looked like the star of a *telenovela*. He was tall, handsome, and smiled reassuringly. At no point did he shame me for subpar brushing or bloated gums. He only asked questions and nodded at my replies.

"The truth is that I am one of the most expensive dentists in Costa Rica," he said. "But I also can offer you excellent quality. I understand if you want to find another practice that is a little bit cheaper, but I think this is the best plan for you."

He described his plan in minute detail: He would remove the three teeth, a surgery that would take only an hour. I would swallow a mild sedative, to ease any anxiety. He would replace the one tooth with a cosmetic substitute—the abscess was infected and would need to heal.

"This replacement is only temporary," said Dr. Anglada. "I will glue the tooth to the teeth around it. Maybe it will last all four months, maybe it will last only a day. I don't know. About fifty percent of my patients lose this type of tooth. But if it falls out, I will replace it right away—for free."

I couldn't believe that a replacement was so easy to install, and told him so.

"Well, it is only for looks," he said. "But I would not let you leave with a missing tooth." Then he guffawed. "It would be very hard to be taken seriously like this, don't you think?"

Yes, I thought, remembering my crabby Pittsburgh dentist. *Imagine that.*

Four months later, Dr. Anglada said, I would receive the same titanium screw that the other dentist had described, and once it had grafted to the bone, he could affix the actual implant.

"This will be a long process," he said. "But if you would like to work with me, I would be happy to do this."

It made me wonder whether my Pittsburgh dentists had ever been happy to do anything. And then the crowning moment: The entire process would cost me about $2,000, over the course of eight months. I could do everything in this office, and Dr. Anglada would perform all surgeries himself. This was an enormous sum for a youngish writer, but it was *exactly* the same price quoted back in the States. Not cheaper, but much easier and more attentive—and with a nationally recognized dental surgeon. To afford the U.S. equivalent, I would have to be a millionaire.

"You will not feel any pain at all," reassured Dr. Anglada, moments before he sawed my tooth in half and yanked its remains out of my face.

I felt calm overall, but two apprehensions dogged me: First, I had to stay awake through the entire procedure, fully conscious of what was happening. Both my wife and I had enjoyed general anesthesia during our wisdom tooth operations. Now I could hear the saw blade whizzing in my ears.

My second apprehension was far more frustrating: My entire life, I had been trained to fear any healthcare outside the United States. In the Gringo worldview, any surgery that takes place beyond our borders must be performed with rusty gardening tools in a bamboo shack. We picture endless lines, floors smeared with blood, greasy rags to blot the wounds. This myth must persevere in order for U.S. healthcare to appear sane. As long as we presume foreign physicians are barbaric, we never question privatized medicine.

"The first one is out," Dr. Anglada said triumphantly.

I was in awe; all I had heard was a crackling noise. All I had felt was pressure, then release. I didn't feel one iota of pain. The removal was so effortless that I almost looked forward to the second one.

The teeth all came out in about 45 minutes, and Dr. Anglada offered comforting words throughout. "You are making this very easy for me," he said. "You are very calm. Not every patient is so calm as you."

Perhaps Dr. Anglada said this to all his patients, even the ones he had to tranquilize, but I was grateful for some cheerleading. When the final tooth came out, I felt some patient's remorse. *It's gone now*, I thought. *I had that tooth my entire life, and now it's gone forever.*

When his assistant came to glue the temporary tooth into place, she examined several sizes of teeth and grinned when she found the right one. The tooth felt weird—a little long and crusty with glue—but I was relieved to have it. When we met Dr. Anglada in his personal office, he told Kylan that I was "very brave." This is not a descriptor I hear often, and in my post-surgery haze I felt positively valiant.

It was strange to pay Dr. Anglada the equivalent of $900 in cash, and stranger still to watch him count it, piling 10,000-*colón* bills on his desk. But this was the one flaw of a Central American office: They charged a five percent fee for credits cards. I decided that visiting the ATM three different times was a small price to pay. (So to speak.)

A week passed after the surgery, and the painkillers and bags of ice worked wonders. My wife gleefully fed me antibiotics, delighted that I had finally acquiesced. The gaping holes in my gums had started feel to feel normal, and the temporary tooth remained intact. According to Dr. Anglada, my premolar had collapsed because of a flawed filling—the only filling I ever had—and my remaining teeth were in excellent condition. In four months, I would return for my titanium screw, and four months after that, my brand new prosthesis: a ceramic tooth fashioned by German engineers.

One night, my wife and I treated ourselves to Pizza Hut. We had enjoyed months of *gallo pinto* and fresh fruit, but we yearned for something greasy and familiar. Halfway through my first slice, I realized that I felt no pain at all. I couldn't use the temporary tooth to chew, but neither did I have to wince. And with that realization, I flashed a big, toothy smile.

Pirates of the Caribbean

When the riverboat hummed its way to the dock, the sky was navy blue. It was 5:15 a.m., and dawn had not yet broken over the dense forests of Tortuguero. A crowd of people waited on the bank, and as they climbed aboard, dumping their bags and taking seats, it was clear there wouldn't be space for all of us.

"They're getting another boat," one backpacker called to the rest of us.

We all nodded. There was nowhere to buy coffee, and most of us were deliriously tired. My wife and I sat on a bench, watching as boatmen pushed the craft free, using a two-by-four for leverage. The river's skin rippled beneath its hull, the outboard motor roared to life, and the dark water boiled around the stern. Within minutes, the boat had vanished into a fine mist.

I scanned the horizon. The sky bloomed red around the silhouette of canopy. There was no sound but the call of birds. The scene was tranquil—just as you'd expect of a remote village in the heart of a rainforest. But I was uneasy. I didn't worry about jaguars or pit vipers or caimans. I knew they lurked out there in the black woods, but they didn't trouble me. We had stood within arm's length of deadly animals only the day before. No problem.

My fear: pirates.

I wanted to take Kylan to Tortuguero for her birthday, because friends had gushed about the northern Caribbean region and Nature Air was running a promotion on one-way flights. We could fly there for cheap, stay in a quaint *cabina*, walk around the village, and paddle a canoe through the legendary canals. It wasn't turtle season, so we couldn't expect to see our first leatherback, but if we liked Tortuguero, we could always come back in

September. In the end, we would take public transit back to San José. Perfect.

Before I left, I mentioned our itinerary to my friend Zach. His smile faded. "You're not taking the bus back, are you?"

"Yeah. We're flying in and bussing out. Why?"

"Are you going through Cariari?"

"I think so."

"Oh. You know about…" He hesitated. "You know about the robberies there, right?"

"I heard about that. But they happened awhile ago, didn't they?"

He frowned. Zach is a journalist who frequently writes about crime for *The Tico Times*, and he related what he'd heard: Because there is no road to Tortuguero, departing tourists must ride riverboats through the canals until they reach a parking lot. From there, a bus takes passengers down a narrow road toward the town of Cariari de Guápiles. The region is filled with banana plantations, and according to reports, farmers occasionally open their large gates and forget to close them. This causes the buses to stop, and sometimes, when they do, masked men leap out of the foliage and threaten the drivers with pistols. They stick up the tourists, steal their valuables, and flee into the fields.

"But I'm sure you'll be fine," Zach said tentatively.

This was not the first bad news I'd heard about Tortuguero. The previous December, three masked assailants overtook a riverboat and robbed 14 people aboard. Technically, it was an act of piracy, and the attackers were never brought to justice. The event was so shocking that locals were worried about its effects on tourism. Tortuguero has no other major industry, and without its steady influx of backpackers and eco-tourists, the town could experience a serious decline.

Costa Rica's Caribbean coast has the country's most unnerving crime statistics. Kylan and I had spent a great deal of time in the country, but we had never visited the Caribbean coast. Kylan's birthday would be our first venture. The last thing I wanted was to have our weekend ruined by a gang of buccaneers in ski masks.

But was there really a problem? If we hadn't known about Tortuguero's crime wave, the village would have seemed perfectly sweet. The first thing they tell you is that Tortuguero has no cars, but really there are no motor vehicles at all. No motorcycles rumble. No trucks or jeeps jostle down the way. Instead of streets, the village is crisscrossed with narrow dirt paths. I had heard of places like this, and as someone who hates driving, I loved the idea. But walking those paths in person was a strange experience. The only engine noise came from the river, where boats hummed across still water.

We also noticed the multitude of roving children, who pedaled bicycles and ate ice cream in the playgrounds and generally seemed as carefree as the exotic birds. Even in the middle of the night, kids would wander around in their dust-matted clothes, strutting in and out of buildings like they owned the place. If a gangly 10-year-old *chiquita* felt safe here, why shouldn't we?

Still, a reputation can cast a shadow over everything, and we couldn't help but approach Tortuguero with silent caution. Yes, we signed up for a night hike and ventured into the dark with a small group. Yes, we rode a canoe into the jungle with our guide, armed with nothing more than handmade paddles. We walked the beach, which was generally empty. We walked the dark paths at night, even after a few beers, knowing full well that an armed mugger could take our stuff and disappear, and we'd probably never catch him. The risks didn't stop us, but the aura of danger wafted everywhere. Such is the power of a headline.

"They just say it's dangerous because a boat was attacked in December," grumbled one tour guide. "That kind of thing almost never happens."

"I take that route to Cariari all the time," said his *compañero* soothingly. "Nothing has ever happened. People take that trip every day. It's very safe."

The problem was not the *probability* of crime—which was extremely low—but the very *possibility* that it could happen, and in such an isolated place. The Judicial Investigation Police (OIJ) has no office in Tortuguero, and although security exists, we had little idea whom to contact if anything went wrong. One of the biggest complaints on the Caribbean coast is that the police aren't very effective. After a shooting in Puerto Viejo wounded five people five months earlier, witnesses said it took officers 30 minutes to respond, and some victims ended up driving themselves to a nearby clinic (they hit a pedestrian on the way). There aren't a lot of shootings in Costa Rica, so when such violence happens, it becomes major news. (Statistically, Costa Ricans are most vulnerable in their own homes, where domestic violence is alarmingly common.) But Ticos and tourists alike tend to lack faith in small-town police—especially in a place as sequestered as Tortuguero.

So we took the usual precautions, hiding our passports and deeply pocketing our cash. We spent little time on obscure paths at night. If something happened, at least we'd done our best to stay safe.

Yet I still felt hypersensitive to peril. Early one morning, a tottering man mumbled, "*Buenos días,*" as we passed. Then he added, in heavily accented English, "Good morning."

"*Hola,*" I said, passing him.

"Hey!" he growled to my back. "Good *morning.*"

I turned around and faced him. The man was ragged and had probably been drinking all night. "Good morning!" I replied, in my airiest, friendliest voice.

The response seemed to satisfy him, and he slinked away. Normally I wouldn't care much about a touchy old codger, but because of our vigilance, the moment was jarring.

After a full day with our own guide, Abel, I finally decided to ask him about crime in Tortuguero. It felt like a tactless question: *Is your hometown as crazy dangerous as people say it is?* But Abel was forthcoming.

"There has been some crime," Abel said. "There is a big problem with drugs in Tortuguero. Marijuana, cocaine, and another one. I don't know the name in English." He used the Spanish term.

"Crack?" Kylan asked.

"That's it! *Piedra.* There are a lot of people who use drugs, and they need money. That's why there's crime in Tortuguero. So yes, sometimes it can be dangerous."

We weren't naïfs, of course. Kylan and I had visited some sketchy places, and we'd had our share of scrapes. We'd been lucky, overall, and grateful for that luck.

The thing is, it only takes one bad moment to cause long-lasting damage. My friend Alejo was born in Costa Rica, but he spent significant time in Mexico City. He recently told me one of the most horrifying stories I've ever heard from a close friend: During a walk in a public park with his then-girlfriend and another friend, a man threatened the trio with a gun. The attacker tied and bound Alejo and his girlfriend, then sexually assaulted their friend. When they notified the authorities, the police were useless. There was no rape kit, no reliable report, not even comforting words. Traumatized and angry, Alejo left Mexico soon after.

"When you talk about traveling alone," Alejo told me, "I just think: I won't do that anymore. It's just too much."

After two action-packed days, we boarded the backup riverboat for Cariari. Color warmed the sky, and individual trees emerged in the forest. We motored down the canal, then veered into a narrow waterway. The muddy banks pressed toward us on either side, and dense vegetation loomed all around. A heavyset man dozed across from me. Belgian backpackers we'd met the night before snapped photos of toucans. Now and again, a submerged tree trunk would scrape along the bottom, or a branch would whip along the gunwales.

If someone attacks us, I thought, *what would I do?*

Because I'm a Gringo, and I was raised on action movies, I immediately envisioned myself engaged in hand-to-hand combat, trying to wrestle a pistol from a terrorist's grip. In our battle for control, the gun would naturally go off, blasting a second attacker in the gut and killing him instantly. There would be lots of punching, until we both tumbled in the water, and a float of caimans would tear the pirate to shreds, eating him on the spot. The backpackers would lift me out of the water, just seconds before a lizard's jaws ripped my legs from my body...

The fantasy was absurd, but the danger seemed all too possible. The creek *is* narrow, and pirates *could* shanghai our boat without much trouble. The sight of a gun would freeze us all, and we would willingly do whatever those attackers commanded. I was almost surprised, after more than two hours of travel, to see the earthen dock, where a queue of smiling tour participants eagerly waited to board.

Next we boarded a bus, and we rode down the very road Zach had warned me about. Indeed, the road was paved with dirt and barely wide enough for two vehicles to pass each other. I saw the rows of banana trees through our windows, with bunches of fruit wrapped in protective bags. I should have found the sight pastoral, but I knew that this particular stretch of road was where travelers had been scared out of their wits. *Nobody was hurt*, I kept reminding myself. *Costa Rica isn't Honduras.*

At last the bus pulled into Cariari, a nondescript town with two different bus stations. We helped our new Belgian friends figure out their connection, and soon we were riding another bus to Guápiles. The road ahead had no reputation, no nightmare tales of highwaymen or ambush.

"I didn't want to mention this before," I finally told the Belgians, as our bus bombed down the well-paved highway, "but there have been some robberies on the road we just took."

"The one back there?" they asked soberly.

"Yeah." I told them what I'd heard. It sounded so silly now, like a ghost story.

"It seemed all right to me," said one of the Belgians.

It did. But then again, it always does.

Moving Pictures

"Try this one on," said the energetic young costumer. She handed me an earth-toned blazer. I slipped my arms through the sleeves and was relieved that it fit perfectly.

"What's your pant size?" she asked, raking through a free-standing rack of clothes.

"I'm not exactly sure," I said. "In the U.S., I'm a 34 waist."

The costumer nodded and went to fetch more options. I stood there, in the corner of a locker room, wondering who exactly I was supposed to be. The last I heard, I would be playing a "Gringo reporter"—which I figured would be easy, since I'm a Gringo reporter in real life. But now I wasn't sure. No one had explained my role. I hadn't even seen a script, much less read it. Then again, that's how movies often work, especially for actors hired at the last minute.

I sat down on a bench. The locker room was buried inside Colleya Fonseca Stadium in Barrio Guadalupe. It was a stuffy antechamber that buzzed with activity. A dozen male actors were dressing themselves in knee socks and athletic shorts, bright jerseys and cleats. Half of them wore the uniforms of the 1990 Costa Rican national soccer team, while the other half dressed in the jerseys of Scotland. Every actor was Tico, and everyone spoke Spanish. Everyone but me—the only Gringo, and the only guy asked to wear a suit.

This was the set of *Italia 90*, a feature-length film produced entirely by a Costa Rican cast and crew. Directed by Miguel Gómez and shot over the course of 20 days, the film's first phase was nearly finished by the time I showed up: The next morning, shooting was slated to wrap.

As I shimmied into a pair of tan slacks, I spotted Alejandra Vargas, the peppy young woman who had hired me. "They need you in makeup," she said. "When you're ready."

Alejandra led me into the dark corridor, which was even busier than the locker room. Crewmembers adjusted lights and tinkered with audio equipment. Actors milled around, pouring themselves coffee and water from plastic containers. Other actors formed a line around the makeup artist. One by one, they sat down, received a dusting of base, and jogged away. Finally I sat down before the middle-aged man and his makeup kit. He held his brush aloft.

"Who are you?" he asked.

Good question, I thought. *I'm not exactly sure.*

Three months earlier, I received an email from deleFOCO, an "audiovisual community" that brings together industry talents from across Central America. The email was a casting call for the film *Italia 90*. The name meant nothing to me, but as a longtime semi-professional actor, I was intrigued. I sent an email to deleFOCO, describing myself as a red-bearded Gringo with passable Spanish and a lot of acting experience. If I wasn't right for *Italia 90*, maybe I could join a roster for future projects?

To my surprise, Alajandra wrote me back a few weeks later to ask for a headshot. Soon after, she offered to put me in a scene as a "Gringo reporter." The prospect excited me, but there was a problem: I was at the beach and couldn't get back in time for the shoot. I assumed I'd missed my chance, but after some phone tag and frantic rescheduling, we finally arranged to shoot a different scene on a sunny April morning.

From the moment I arrived on set, I was impressed: I've worked on only a couple of Hollywood sets, and always as an extra. But the Costa Rican studio had all the essentials—catered breakfast, grips, dressers, makeup people and mountains of equipment, from a professional digital camera to boom mics and floodlights. What really struck me was the costuming: Each actor was outfitted with period-accurate Selección uniforms from 1990, including outrageously short shorts. The actors had fashioned their hair into mullets and Jheri curls. The costumers had even applied colored tape to their socks, to make them appear striped.

"It's so weird," murmured one actor dressed as a referee. "They look just like famous La Sele players. I keep thinking, 'That's Enrique Rivers.' But then I think, 'No, that's just an actor.'"

I laughed and nodded, even though I had no idea who Enrique Rivers was. Until this past year, I had never seen a professional soccer game played in its entirety, and I knew nothing about the history of La Sele. In a way, I was the least likely person to appear in a sports movie, much less a movie about Costa Rican soccer legends. But as I learned more about the project, it became clear how special *Italia 90* would be—not for Gringo reporters, but for Ticos who remembered that fateful year.

By 1989, world soccer fans pretty much ignored La Sele, as Costa Rica's national soccer team is known. While the team had existed since 1921, Costa Rica's players hadn't impressed anyone for two solid decades.

"It's not like today," my friend Beto recently told me. "They had to work regular jobs."

When Costa Rica qualified for the 14th World Cup, they suddenly had a chance to fly to Italy and perform on a global stage. To everyone's surprise, Costa Rica defeated both Scotland *and* Sweden in the first round. The 1990 World Cup was also a blockbuster event—billions of people tuned into the games on television, competition was particularly brutal, and FIFA handed out a record number of red cards.

You could say that 1990 was La Sele's "Rocky" moment: They didn't win the cup, but their success in Italy won international acclaim and boosted Costa Rican confidence. Many would argue that that year was the turning point, and La Sele would never be the popular powerhouse it is today without "Italia 90."

I try to imagine a familiar equivalent: If Pittsburgh (where I lived most of my adult life) produced a movie called *The Immaculate Reception*, produced entirely in Western Pennsylvania and starring respected local actors, movie theaters would overflow with Steelers fans. The nostalgia and pride would excite everyone who remembered—or had even heard of—that miraculous play in 1972.

For Ticos, *Italia 90* isn't just a movie: It's a chance to relive a national triumph.

"Places, everybody!" shouted Santiago Fornaguera, the tough and humorless assistant director of *Italia 90*. "*¡Vamos! ¡Vamos! ¡Rápido!*"

As a rule, filmmaking is torturously slow, and most time is spent quietly hanging around. (I once spent two entire days bumming around a parking lot, waiting for someone to use me in a scene. I spent nearly 18 hours doing nothing but working up the courage to say hi to Maggie Gyllenhaal.) In the stuffy corridor of the Colleya Fonseca Stadium, the set was filled with the usual anarchy: cinematographers adjusting the camera, technicians debating how to light the scene, and lots of unidentified assistants scrambling around. To a director, all this stuff makes sense. To a random extra, it's bedlam.

But then the two teams lined up, side by side. At the rear of the line stood a skinny actor in a polo shirt. As we waited for the production team to set up, the actor made small talk with me in fluent English.

"I'm playing Bora Milutinovic," he said. "He was the Ticos' coach in 1990. Really interesting guy. He brought five different teams to the World Cup. He was a real inspiration to the players." He added, "At the end of the shot, I'm supposed to lean into you and say, 'These guys are like my kids.' It's not in the script, but they want to show that moment."

"Lean into *me?*" I said.

"Yeah. Because you're the Scottish coach."

I smiled at this, but I wanted to double over laughing. *The Scottish coach?* It didn't really matter who I was, since I had no lines, but I loved the idea of standing in for such a dignified personality. Did the real Scottish coach of 1990 have a red beard? Was he in his mid-thirties? Did I look *anything like him?*

For a few minutes we joked about how much fun it would be to say some lines in a terrible Scottish accent, but our joviality was interrupted by Fornaguera. "Positions, everyone!" he shouted. "And... *action!*"

The scene was brief, but it was significant: Moments before the two teams enter the field, the Ticos start shit-talking their Scottish rivals. They yell insults and gruffly chant. One of the players starts to drag his shoes across concrete, and sparks fly from his cleats. (The sparks were a special effect, but they looked fearsome.) Then the enormous gates open, and the two teams march forward, into blinding daylight.

As film roles go, the "Scottish coach" was almost meaningless, and I might as well have played the soccer ball. But I was thrilled to contribute, in my own tiny way, to a Costa Rican film. Over the course of three hours, I sensed the camaraderie of the crew; aside from one Venezuelan, everyone seemed to be born and raised in Costa Rica. Almost everyone appeared old enough to remember the Italian World Cup. The operation felt tight and professional. In such a small country, where feature films are rare and small-budget, I loved the attention to detail: The crew filmed the scene from every angle. When actors started to drag, we received cookies and cups of coffee.

Like most movie shoots, the session ended without fanfare. "You're done," said Alejandra. "You can go now."

I changed into my regular clothes and left the stadium, heading for the nearest bus stop. I was lightheaded and my body ached, as often happens after making the same motions 20 times in a row, with long stretches between takes. But I was happy I'd made it. I had made my Latin American debut during a critical period in the Costa Rican film industry. I would probably be a fuzzy silhouette in the background. I might be cut altogether. But the experience was totally worth a few hours on a Thursday.

Before I left, Alejandra revealed the film's astonishing timetable: "We want to release the film before the World Cup." That is, within five weeks.

Few features are put together so quickly, and most "post" sessions can take months or even a year. Yet I soon learned that the *Italia 90* team had shot footage each day and then edited the scenes the very same night. Unlike Hollywood films, Costa Rican producers don't get bogged down in the studio system, appeasing focus groups and appealing to the Motion Picture Association for a lower rating. While the coffee giant Café Volio was sponsoring the film, Tico producers don't have to satisfy armies of investors or spend a fortune on publicity. While the film's budget was probably modest (the studio refused to give me an exact figure), such freedom is its own virtue.

When the trailer was released online a few days later, I was delighted. My Tico friends were already excited about the film's official release, when cinemas across Costa Rica would screen *Italia 90*.

"There are several things people don't know about the players or that moment," director Gómez said during an interview with *La Nación*. "They don't really know about how they prepared. The film is about those guys, who are very humble."

It was impossible to say how good *Italia 90* would be. But it didn't really matter. I would just be happy to root for the home team.

Inside the Refugio

A smiley cashier welcomed me in the lobby. His arms were akimbo. He wore a polo shirt that read, "Refugio Herpetológico."

"Welcome!" he exclaimed in Spanish. "How are you?"

I forced a smile and forked over my 3,000 *colones*—about $6. He handed me a receipt and escorted me through the gift shop, toward the Refugio's main entrance. Then he pointed to a trim young man in the corner, also wearing a printed polo shirt.

"This is Marco," said the cashier. "Your tour will start in a couple of minutes."

Damn it, I thought. *It figures.*

As a rule, I don't like tours, especially in places that are essentially museums. After 10 minutes roaming around with a droning docent, all I want to do is take a nap. Their scripted monologues ruin the experience, especially when there are printed plaques that already explain everything. With his samurai ponytail and acne-scarred skin, Marco looked like a congenial kid, but I wanted nothing to do with him.

Still, I had missed my chance to visit the Refugio for eight months. Ever since I moved to Costa Rica, I had wondered about this odd little sanctuary in the suburbs of San José, and I had finally found a free Sunday afternoon to visit. If I must tolerate a guide, I would tolerate a guide. If there's one thing I'd learned from Ticos, it's patience.

My tiny group sidled up to a glass box. Its frame was wooden and the ceiling was chicken wire, but basically the space was a glorified aquarium. Two grass-green snakes coiled around each other on a branch. One remained still while the second slid up its back, until their heads were congruent. I half-listened to Marco's speech about the species and its habitat.

"They seem very energetic," I said.

"Energetic?"

"Sometimes animals in captivity stay very still. There isn't much movement. But these two are moving around."

"Yes, it's true," Marco agreed. "It's a very active species. They're usually nocturnal, and they tend to spend time in the trees. Most of the animals here are inoffensive, but they can be very aggressive and dangerous, when humans provoke them."

I had seen *Oxybelis fulgidus* before, in the cloud forests of Santa Elena. I had heard stories of bitten victims cutting off their limbs with machetes to keep the venom from killing them. The snakes looked so pathetic in their glass box, a hundred miles from their relatives in the rainforest.

But I also knew that these glass boxes might be the best option the animals had. As we passed more enclosures, where bored eyelash vipers and boa constrictors lay still, I started taking pictures. And little by little, I started listening to what Marco was saying.

On paper, Costa Rica is a very "green" country. The national parks are enormous. Game hunting is illegal. Vast tracts are dubbed "protected areas." Each claim is flawed, and enforcement is weak, but the Costa Rican government portrays its country as lush, lively, and carbon-neutral, and foreigners generally love it.

In 2013, Costa Rica shocked the world: The Environmental Ministry announced that it would close two public zoos and free the animals. Practically speaking, this meant releasing around 400 creatures into the wild. More sentimentally, it meant shuttering the 100-year-old Zoológico Simón Bolivar in downtown San José, where generations of Ticos had seen their first African lion. And what would happen to that lion? It was hard to say.

The buzz-phrase was "cage-free," and people take it seriously. Protesting animal rights activists had gotten into skirmishes with police over Simón Bolivar. The zoo's staff had fought bitterly in the courtroom for its right to stay open.

When I first moved to Costa Rica, I learned that the zoo would soon close, and because its entrance was located only a few blocks from my office, I decided to spend an afternoon walking its grounds. The day was overcast and spurted rain, and the place looked particularly gloomy. Monkeys lazed on their hemp ropes, and parrots chewed the wire grids of their cages. I saw only two other visitors, a man and woman, who kept feeding fallen leaves to a curious tapir, despite the signs that forbade doing so. I left the zoo with mixed feelings, but mostly I looked forward to its dignified demise.

False hope, it turned out. In early 2014, the zoo found a legal loophole, and a court ruled in their favor. The zoos won a 10-year contract, and the Environmental Ministry had to go back to the drawing board. The war, it seemed, was far from over.

"These are our spider monkeys," said Marco. He held out a hand, and a nervous ape swung his way over and reached its own arm through the cage's chain-link fence. Human and primate touched fingers, like two old friends. Then the monkey screeched excitedly and darted away. "They are very friendly," Marco added, smiling.

The monkeys were cute, even behind bars. But what were spider monkeys doing in a serpentarium?

In 2003, a certain Rodolfo Vargas Leiton established the Refugio Herpetológico with a simple mission: to rehabilitate amphibians and reptiles and release them back into the wild. The Refugio expanded rapidly, and in 2008 they were forced to move to larger quarters, the location where I was now standing.

On the surface, the place looks like a rundown roadside attraction. Situated on a sloped byway between the suburbs of Escazú and Santa Ana, the Refugio is basically a few hectares of land enclosed by a wire fence covered in green plastic. As trucks and buses fly past, the tarp perimeter whips in the wind. The walls are covered in cheesy murals; above the crocodile tank rises a landscape of pharaohs and pyramids. The interior looks like a rainforest, and concrete walkways crisscross the trees and bushes, but parts of the Refugio look makeshift and low-rent, like a landscaped backyard.

"How much food do your animals have to eat?" I finally asked Marco. The subject interested me, because I had once toured the kitchen of the National Aviary, back in Pittsburgh, and I was stunned by the volume of worms, insects, and frozen chicks.

"It depends on the animals," Marco said, suddenly animated. "But this crocodile, for example, eats about four chickens a day."

As we passed cages for owls and toucans, I felt increasingly annoyed. The Refugio seemed to have a very loose idea of "herpetology," and despite its leafy surface, the place looked cramped. Legally, the Refugio and the zoos are completely different animals: While the zoo is a public institution that puts wildlife on display, a "rescue center" is designed to rehabilitate wildlife and eventually let them run free. Yet a rescue center can do everything a zoo does: charge an entrance fee, lead tours, and show off their menageries.

Two girls in my tour group posed in front of a rainbow-hued macaw. Unlike the other birds, the macaws were "free," in the sense that their wings were clipped and they could openly wander the Refugio grounds. Each time one girl posed, clutching her hips and smiling like a model, the bird behind her turned around, flaring its feathers. It looked like the bird was mooning the camera, and both girls burst into giggles.

That about sums it up, I thought.

I feel the same way about animal rights that I feel about Israel or abortion: total philosophical stalemate. I don't like to see animals in captivity, and I would rather they lived and died without human involvement. In theory, a spider monkey with a head-injury should face its Darwinian fate, and bleeding-heart veterinarians should lay off. But with seven billion humans clogging the world, wild habitats may need every break they can get. Costa Rica is crawling with wildlife profiteers, from illegal fishermen to turtle-egg poachers to trappers of exotic birds. If a loving biologist can save an animal in the short term, why not?

But I have a hard time distinguishing between a "rescue center" and a zoo, since they behave almost identically. Costa Rica has plenty of wilderness, and for the most part, the government enthusiastically celebrates those open spaces. Tico naturalists are the only guides I enjoy, because they are rigorously trained and passionate about their work. In the rainforest, anything can happen, yet seasoned naturalists always know where to look. They are the greatest improvisers I've ever met, turning just the right leaf to reveal just the right tree frog. In Tortuguero, my guide tracked a venomous snake from 300 meters *because he could smell it*.

Why, then, is Costa Rica also home to Africa Mia, a synthetic African safari in Guanacaste, where tourists can drive through herds of zebra and giraffes? Why is there a gigantic "sloth sanctuary" in Limón Province, where tourists pay $25 to hang out with the world's slowest mammals, complete with jungle boat ride? There's nothing wrong with these places; the sloths living on a 300-acre property don't seem exactly "caged." But the arrangement still puts me ill at ease.

For concerned environmentalists, each location is a triumph for wildlife. Not only do they get to rescue endangered animals, but the operation is also sustainable—tourists will pay handsomely just to show up and look an anteater in the eye. Yet the rescue centers are also a sign of global failure: They prove that natural spaces are critically handicapped. The ecosystem can't survive without human maintenance, and human maintenance can't survive without a decent gift shop to fund it.

As the other guests took pictures, I finally took Marco aside and asked him my burning question.

"I know there's been a lot of conflict between the zoos and the government," I said. "So what exactly is the difference between the Refugio and the zoos?"

Marco nodded understandingly. I was worried he would get defensive, and I wouldn't understand the reply, because hostile Spanish is the hardest for me to follow. But Marco turned even more serious and delivered his explanation: "A zoo displays animals, and the animals live there their entire lives. The purpose of a zoo is to keep the animals in cages. Here, no animals stay longer than they have to. The only reason we show them to people is to educate them. We are here so people can learn. Many of these animals are sick, and we receive all of them from the government. But it's about education."

Marco blinked, in the stoic way that Ticos often use to say, *That's it. Your turn.*

"*Claro*," I said. "*Entiendo*."

That wasn't quite true. I still felt the distinction was foggy, and I wondered whether Sea World might also be considered "educational." But I liked that Marco was so unapologetic. He was young and straightforward, and he clearly cared about the animals. In total, the tour lasted two hours. He spoke intelligently about each animal, and he admitted when he didn't know something. ("What do you do with the snake skins?" I asked him. "I'm not sure exactly," Marco replied, but then he waxed poetic on serpentine molting.)

As we approached the final cages of iguanas and squirrel monkeys, I felt more forgiving of the Refugio. The place lacked some polish, and it would function just as well as a South Dakota highway attraction. But superficial judgments aside, Marco sounded as sharp and professional as any wilderness guide I had met. He knew how to hold a scorpion turtle shell so that the head wouldn't shoot out and bite his finger off. When he called the simians by name, they turned their heads and squealed.

One cage seemed empty. A placard read "Manigordo" in Spanish, then the English translation: "Ocelot." Also called a "dwarf leopard," the ocelot looks like an overgrown housecat with patterned fur. We all leaned toward the cage, trying to see the wild feline inside, but nothing stirred. The ocelot had clearly retreated into a pipe or behind a tree.

"The ocelot is nocturnal," said Marco. "Most visitors never see it."

The shadows of foliage painted the soil. It felt silly, standing in a line and gazing at nothing. But still we stood there, looking at the empty space, waiting for nature to do something.

Bioluminescent in Bocas

As we stumbled aboard the motorboat, I realized that I had never really ventured into the ocean at night. At 7 p.m., the Bay of Almirante was a vast expanse of darkness dotted with distant lights. The rickety dock rocked beneath my Keens as I stepped clumsily into the boat. A lukewarm breeze seeped across our skin, having passed across that endless, invisible surface.

"Are you nervous?" I asked Erin.

"No," she said. "Are you?"

"Yeah, actually." I sat down in the crowded boat and fiddled with an antiquated orange life preserver. "The water looks a lot different when you can't see it."

The captain was a stout Panamanian named Jorge, and when he started the engine, he used its noise as an excuse to sing love songs at the top of his lungs. The boat angled forward, and once we were clear of the dock, we launched into the void.

We didn't know exactly where we were going or how the boat ride would transpire. We had only just met our guide, Jon, a skinny guy with long blonde hair who looked no older than 18. We weren't even sure how long we'd be putting around the bay.

Only one thing was certain: Within the next couple hours, we would get to swim with bioluminescent phytoplankton, one of the most mystifying forms of marine life.

"I need to get out of town for a few days," I told Erin, my colleague at *The Tico Times* and one of my favorite people to travel with. "Any interest in going to Bocas?"

"Yes!" she said. "I've been *dying* to go there!"

Most folks in Costa Rica know that Bocas del Toro is a kooky little province in the northwestern corner of Panama, a region famous for secluded islands, sprawling mangroves, and red tree frogs. Known among fans as simply "Bocas," the main settlement is an old company town metamorphosed into a tourist mecca. The islands were once vassals of the United Fruit Company. Today, the place is overrun with backpackers and retirees from other countries.

While plenty of millionaires vacation in Bocas, the place has a countercultural flavor: Gringo's Mexican is a quirky little restaurant run by a chatty Californian expat. Bocas Blended is a cute eatery built into a retired truck. Erin and I booked a room at Mar e Iguana, a hostel on the outskirts of town. When the *taxista* drove us there, he pulled up to the beach, pointed to the hostel's entrance, and said, "*Estamos aquí. Mar e Iguana.*"

"Oh, my God," I exclaimed as we (gently) closed the taxi's doors. "I didn't even get that."

"Get what?"

"The name of this place."

"What about it?"

"Say it fast and don't pronounce the 'g.'"

"What? *Marijuana?*" As she said this, Erin's jaw dropped, and we burst into cackles.

As it happened, Mar e Iguana was a tame—not to mention beautiful—little hostel, and most of its denizens were young Germans on their *Wanderjahr*. Bocas del Toro has its share of parties and reckless behavior, but a critical mass of visitors comes for more than cheap Balboa beer and ubiquitous ganja. They want to also lie on isolated beaches, go snorkeling near dolphin pods, and climb into caves full of bats. They want to rent bicycles and pedal down jungle roads, or hike the trails of Red Frog Beach and admire the exotic birds.

The punishing heat of Bocas made any plan seem pointless, so Erin and I alternated between hammocks, beaches, seafood restaurants and bars. Bocas can feel very far from real life, especially if you spend most of your time in Costa Rica: You have to cross the trestle bridge at Sixaola, take buses or a cab to the coast, then board a water taxi and thread your way between the islands. Sometimes the water shuts off or the electricity cuts out. Wifi is patchy, and we never found an Internet café. These inconveniences are all part of Bocas del Toro's freewheeling charm, and we found excuse after excuse not to do anything meaningful.

Then, during one of our long strolls through town, we found a handwritten sign: BIOLUMINESCENT TOURS. We had both seen this phenomenon before, but only in small doses. We talked with a drowsy-looking girl from California named Taylor, who described the tour.

"It's about three hours long," she said. "We take you out in a boat, and you get to see the algae. Then you get to jump in and swim around with masks. It's really amazing." Then she looked up at the opal sky and added, "Tonight is the new moon, which means it's *the best night of the month to see it*."

Taylor started the tour about a year earlier, and she had continued its operation with her boyfriend Jon, who was born in Holland but raised in Panama. What was striking about the tour was its price tag: $25 U.S. Like so many activities in Central America, some parts of Bocas del Toro are best visited with guides—and many of these tours are cheap and easy.

"So I brought a GoPro with me," I told Taylor. "Do you think it'll work?"

"Honestly," she said, "I'd say don't bother. People take cameras all the time, and all they get is a black screen. There *are* ways to take pictures of bioluminescent algae, but only if you're an expert. Like a *National Geographic* photographer probably could, and I've seen pictures online, but most of us can't. So you're welcome to bring it along, but I'm pretty sure you're not going to get anything."

We booked two seats on the boat, grabbed some pad thai, and headed to the hostel to fetch our swimsuits. Within a few hours, the sun had set and we were ready to sail.

Jorge veered the boat sideways, and we started motoring into a tight circle. As water riffled along the hull, we could see thousands of faint specs light up in the liquid furrows.

"This is the bioluminescent phytoplankton," said Jon triumphantly.

With the exception of fireflies and glowworms, bioluminescence is a rare sight in the terrestrial world. Mammals and reptiles generally have no need to glow in the dark, so when the lights go out, so do we. But underwater, bioluminescence is a common phenomenon, and the more fathoms you descend, the more glowing creatures you'll find. There are lots of reasons that critters have evolved to share this treat, from intimidating predators to lighting their way in the Mariana Trench.

Yet nothing is quite as startling as bioluminescent phytoplankton. Aroused by movement, this algae forms galactic patterns in the water.

"Scientists call them *dinoflagellates*," shouted Jon over the roar of the engine.

"Now *that's* a name!" someone shouted back, and everybody laughed.

There were about a dozen of us, and all of us were youngish—no one older than 35. As members of the digital generation, most of the passengers started frantically shooting the water with their cameras and phones, trying to capture images of the algae. Flashes burst blindingly in the dark, but when the snapshots registered on their screens, they showed only blackness or abstract light patterns.

"Seriously, guys," said Jon in his surfer-dude cadence. "You're not going to get a picture of them, especially with flash. You're just making it harder for other people to see."

At first the algae was subtle, and Erin and I kept murmuring our disappointment.

"I really don't see much," she said. "It's just like a couple of dots."

Then the boat drifted into the mangroves, and Jorge switched off the engine. He and Jon handed paddles and wood poles down the aisles of seats, and each of us dipped our implements in the water. With each swish of a paddle, algae bubbled around like heaps of diamonds. "Oh, wow!" we cooed, because there was nothing else to say. Words were as ineffectual as camera lenses.

"So are we swimming here?" someone called to Jon.

"Not here," Jon said. "Back in the bay."

"Why not here?"

"Look around," Jon said, gesturing to the curtains of trees and foliage that hung over the water. "It's *creepy*." Again, everyone laughed. "Also, this is where lots of fish come to feed, and they're attracted to the bioluminescence. But sharks come to eat the fish. So the chances of a shark attacking you are point-zero-zero-zero-zero-one percent. But where we're going, we'll be perfectly safe."

Anchored off an island the size of a baseball mound, we slipped off the boat into the unseen water. One by one, bodies vanished into the shadows, and then heads popped back up, spitting water and crying, "Oh, it's cold!"

But I adjusted quickly to the tropical water, delighted to taste salt on my lips. Jon advised us to stay on the surface, for fear we'd touch the bottom and impale our feet on a sea urchin. I felt buoyant and free, and I spent long minutes floating on my back, watching the starry cosmos rotate above.

"Mask?" someone called out.

"Here!" I called back.

I strapped on the rubber mask and dipped my face into the ripples. Just as Taylor predicted, glowing particles swarmed around my hands. The tiniest wiggle of my thumb caused sparks to swirl. Kicking my feet raised clouds of algae, and when I ran fingers through my chest hair, specs lit up.

"Erin..." I said, ripping off the mask and handing it off.

"This... is... *awesome*..." Erin intoned, once she'd come up for breath.

As we dog-paddled around the boat, unafraid of the obscure depths, lost in the wonder of the moment, it occurred to me how spoiled a visitor can become in Central America. Things that once seemed to exist only in magazines—sloths, cloud forests, waterfalls descending into jungle ravines—are everyday sights in Costa Rica. Surfing and scuba diving once seemed hopelessly exotic, but in recent months I've been able to try either on a whim.

Indeed, bioluminescent phytoplankton is fairly common, and not just in Panama: Backpackers later told me about blooms off the coast of Nicoya, which they claimed were visible from the beach.

But as we climbed awkwardly back into the boat, reluctant to leave our dark patch of illuminated life, I hoped never to let that novelty wear off. Part of what makes places like Costa Rica and Panama so wondrous, especially for people who grew up elsewhere, is the richness of its species. Even hardened urban Yankees come to Latin America and wander around the national parks, slack-jawed, because every little bug enthralls them.

Erin and I returned to land, spent a few hours at a bar, and gabbed with a bunch of fellow travelers.

"What have you done?" they asked, in various ways and in various accents.

"We just got back from the bioluminescent tour," we gushed. "And *it is amazing.*"

The next day, the hostel's water cut out. Already sweat-matted, we trekked through the sweltering heat, all the way back to Sixaola. As we scrambled aboard the bus for San José—only minutes before its departure—Erin smiled broadly and said, "Hey, I'm still covered in bioluminescent phytoplankton. How about you?"

"Yeah," I said. "I guess I am."

That's the thing about nature: It sticks with you.

La Temporada Verde

How to Survive the Rainy Season

1. Buy an umbrella. You will laugh at first. *An umbrella? Who am I, Mary Poppins?* But it will only take one rainstorm in San José to realize how important an umbrella is. Your expensive, collapsible rain jacket will be useless; the downpour will soak through its nylon fabric. By the time you reach your front door, you'll feel like you barely survived a shipwreck.

2. Seek cover. The city is filled with awnings and covered walkways, and you will scramble from one roof to the next in search of dry pavement. But because crowds gather beneath them, you'll get pushed to the edge of the sidewalk, which is the worst place to stand: The water falls heaviest here, slicked off the edges of roofs and shooting out of drain pipes. When in doubt, just huddle with a group of pedestrians against a storefront, nibble an empanada, and wait.

3. Disbelieve how loud the rain can be. It pounds the corrugated rooftops, rakes through palm leaves, smashes against pavement, gurgles along the gutters, sizzles down rain chains, smacks into buckets, and roars across the skyline. Then the thunder starts, rumbling slowly over the horizon.

4. Listen to the thunder. When lightning strikes near your apartment, the crash of cosmic electricity will make you jump off the couch. Hear yourself yelp with surprise. Laugh self-consciously as your pulse returns to normal.

5. Avoid the puddles. The streets bend in unusual ways, and deluges surge through the gutters, erasing them from sight. At any moment, a bus could charge through the water, raising geysers of brown water. And watch your step—you could fall into one of those trenches, immerse your pant leg, and sprain an ankle.

6. Wait for buses in the rain. Stand in the open street, because too many people are crammed under the bus stop shelter. Your umbrella will seem hopelessly small. Feel the rain pour all around you, dampening your pant legs and backpack. When you hobble aboard the bus, note how every plastic seat is pooled with water. Wipe the water onto the floor with a cupped hand, then give up and sit down on the droplets.

7. Shake out your umbrella when you reach your office, then open it completely and leave it on the front stoop to dry. Forget it there almost every day, then curse yourself a few blocks up the hill when it's too inconvenient to turn around. Get rained on a few minutes later.

8. Wonder how the sun could shine so bright, and yet the rain could fall so heavily.

9. Watch your contact lenses fog up. Watch your camera lens fog up. Watch every window and windshield mist over until drivers can barely see where they're going. Anxiously ponder how anybody can drive in San José traffic while unable to see through the obscured glass and sheets of rain.

10. Jam three sets of clothes into your backpack—a T-shirt that you can sweat through, a collared shirt you can wear during the day, and running gear.

11. Forget the word "umbrella." Say *paraguas*, even when otherwise speaking in English, because the word just rolls off the tongue. ¡*Paraguas!*

12. Accept that your shoes will get wet. Ignore their squeak as you march down the asphalt. Sigh at your shoelaces, which flop heavily over your toe.

13. Relish hot showers. Once you strip off your dripping outfit, letting the layers clump on the bathroom tile, the steamy stream from your showerhead will soothe you like a thermal bath.

14. Remember autumn days in the Northeast. Stock up on Turrialba cheese and wheat bread and cans of tomato soup. Dip grilled cheese sandwiches into your soup bowl as you zip up your hoodie. Consider visiting the sports bar down the street and asking to watch an American football game on their TV.

15. Remember winter. Spend a shocking amount of time watching movies on Netflix. Read shelves full of books. Listen to music mixes on 8Tracks. Wash enormous loads of laundry. Make excessive amounts of coffee and green tea. Snack on plantain chips as you wander from room to room, lost in thought. Finish the bag and wonder where all the plantain chips went.

16. Get cabin fever. Mix *guaro* and fruit juice in a glass.

17. Talk about the weather. When you've run out of the usual *taxista* topics—soccer, crime, women—talk about how much you're looking forward to the dry season. "Oh, it's much nicer in December," the *taxista* will agree. "But the rainy season mornings are nice."

18. Don't let the rainy season deceive you. Oh, it's bright and sunny in the morning, and the clouds are puffy and white until noon. But then they condense, darken, and drown out the sky. First come the heavy droplets, pecking the pavement, followed by a light and steamy drizzle. Then the rainfall thickens, the temperature drops, and everything gets murky

and gray. Minutes roll into hours, and the rain keeps tumbling down. If you have nowhere to go; if you're sitting in an ergonomic chair in your office; if you're lying on a couch in your living room, you will come to love this sight. How much water can the sky actually dump on a single city? And for how long? It will amaze you every time, and sometimes the rain will keep coming long into the night.

19. Watch the clouds. Notice how they roll over the mountains, like dark gray quilts dragged across the escarpments. First they drape the peaks, the cliffs, the dense forest, then they descend into the valleys, blanketing houses and roads and even nearby electrical lines until your own residential block is murky with fog, and the street lamps are only haloed will-o'-the-wisps in the early night. Spend entire bus rides watching the clouds crawl over mountain ranges or drift through basins. Watch them change color throughout the day, until they zenith with pink and purple at sunset. Wonder if there's any sight as beautiful in the world.

20. Buy a blender. Tentatively fill it with yoghurt, then yoghurt and bananas. Eventually you will stuff the blender with yoghurt, bananas, mangos, pineapple, mixed berries, coconut water, low-sugar fruit juice, hemp seeds, spirulina, soy milk, and ice cubes. Look forward to browsing the supermarket so you can stock up on fruits to liquefy. Wonder why you never owned a blender before. Make milkshakes and hummus. Replace half your meals with blended drinks. Lose some weight. Check yourself out in the mirror. Nod approvingly.

21. Consider taking a yoga class. But plan on really sticking to it this time.

22. Start running home from the office. Stuff your phone and work clothes into a garbage bag so that they stay dry, then seal everything into your backpack. Jog up the hill from Barrio Amón, then dodge walkers on the narrow sidewalks.

Hopscotch through the crowds of Avenida Central, then pick up speed as you run toward La Sabana Park. The rain will come, and lightning will strike intermittently, but allow the rain to drench you, splash in the puddles, ignore your saturated socks. Flaunt your slicked hair, your grime-streaked face, the brown rivulets that dribble down your leg hair. Fight the rain, then embrace it, then love it. Let it cool your sweating body. Study the ever-morphing sky. Slip between idling cars. Smile to passersby, who look astonished that anyone would run five miles through the cloudburst. Do this every afternoon you can.

23. Remember that it's the "green season." Okay, sure, that's what the Tourism Ministry calls it—because the "rainy season" doesn't sound as inviting—but the landscape really *is* green. Trees that looked bent over and dead during the dry season gradually flood with life. The shriveled yellow leaves crumble away, replaced by unfurling green buds. Brown lawns grow dense with grass. When September rolls around, and the rain falls heavier than ever, consider that you've lived in Costa Rica for a year. You are no longer "new" here. You've experienced the rain, you've survived, and you've come to like it. Your life in Central America is its own sort of green season—misty, soggy, slow, and confined, but also abundant with fresh life, verdant with friends and activity, as invigorating indoors as outdoors. Let the rain fall, and watch everything come alive.

Car Trouble

The cab dropped us off at a gas station. The asphalt glowed in the early morning sun. Kylan and I glanced at each other. *Where are we?* read our expressions. We had never visited this part of San José, and we were too groggy to appreciate the new sights. We followed the directions specifically: One hundred meters east of the *gasolinera*. We found the specified corner, and then we stopped and gawked.

We had expected one man and one vehicle—a Jeep Grand Cherokee, parked on the curb. Instead we found two men, wearing camouflage cargo pants and bandannas over their faces, and a Jeep half-covered in tarp. The men glanced at us. They looked like cartel hitmen. Then they went back to work, waxing the exposed half of the car.

The owner appeared, trooping eagerly toward us. Sergio had severe facial features and a receding hairline. He welcomed us briskly and then pointed to the car.

"How do you like it?" he demanded.

"Why is there a tarp?" asked Kylan.

"Oh," he said, and strode over to the car, then lifted the plastic out of the way. "Because of this."

This was a massive concussion in the side of the Jeep. *This* was a bent chassis and two missing doors. *This* was a car that had clearly been T-boned at an intersection, and for whatever reason, Sergio had never fixed it. *This* was damage so serious that we would have to spend thousands of dollars on repairs and replacements before we could even drive it home.

"What do you think?" said Sergio hurriedly.

"There aren't any doors," said Kylan.

"Oh, well, there was in an accident," said Sergio.

"Right, but in the pictures online, it didn't show any missing doors."

Sergio closed his eyes, as if pained by our nitpicking. "I could only upload five pictures. There was a sixth picture that showed this side of the car, but I couldn't upload any more."

"Okay, well, I don't think we're going to take it," said Kylan.

"No?" He looked disappointed that he had wasted his time.

"No. We need a car…" How to describe it? Kylan finished: "We need a car in better condition. Sorry."

He nodded dismissively and mumbled, "*Hasta luego*," then sauntered away.

The only positive side to waking early on a Saturday and schlepping across San José for nothing was that we could post our story on social media. In summary: "The car was perfect, except for the missing doors."

We received a flurry of sarcastic responses on Facebook, from our Costa Rican friends and from friends back in the United States: "Doors are overrated," and, "If you wanted a car that worked, why didn't you say so?" We had a good laugh, but the fact remained that we still had no vehicle.

We had spent nearly a year in Costa Rica, and we had been content to walk and take the bus. Taxis were in ample supply, and for very short distances, I could ride my bicycle. But as much as I loved the Costa Rican transportation system, some destinations were strenuous to reach. I once had to attend a concert at the Pedregal Event Center in Belén, a nondescript suburb northeast of San José. I took a $25 cab to the event; afterward, I waited more than an hour on a dark street corner for a bus to San José, then spent another $10 on a taxi from San José to Escazú. Belén is only about seven miles from my house—I could've walked that distance, if the roads were remotely direct and safe—but in Costa Rica, distance is deceptive.

In every other respect, our lives had exponentially improved in 11 months. We had finally terminated our AT&T contract and started using our iPhones in Costa Rica for a fraction of the U.S. price. We could retire our cheap temporary cell phones and loan them to friends when they visited. Our once empty apartment was gradually accumulating kitchen implements and décor. We even bought items we had never owned, like a wok and a quality grille.

But we only invested in small things, because our Costa Rican life seemed so tenuous. Would our jobs remain intact? Would immigration laws change? Could we sustain our modest network of friends? Each month we felt surer than the last, and our resources felt less piecemeal. Buying a blender was a major step. Could we, in fact, buy a car?

The truth is that I have long feared driving, and I have never bought a serious automotive vehicle. Kylan and I shared her Volvo for several years, and I had overcome my phobia, but actually registering a car with the DMV was a level of commitment I had never considered in the States. To truly enjoy Costa Rica, to really cement ourselves to the country, we had to accrue some wheels. A car would unlock entire chunks of the country that were inaccessible by bus or on foot.

Like most imported items, cars are expensive in Costa Rica. As far as local banks are concerned, expats have no credit history, so there was no way to finance our purchase. We would have to buy a car outright, just as all our foreign friends had done, which meant finding something second-hand.

Kylan was optimistic about finding a car—she loved surfing the Internet and scrolling through pictures—until the doorless Jeep incident. Sergio had singlehandedly soured our trust in online venders. If someone could try to sell us a car with vital components so obviously absent, what else could be missing or broken that we wouldn't discover until we were bombing down the highway at 100 kilometers per hour?

What's more, Costa Ricans don't just sell each other things. They require an attorney to file the paperwork, and oftentimes the attorney actually creates a company name—on behalf the client—in order to register the car. In other words, if you see a well-off Tico 20-year-old cruising around in a Lexus, he might be the CEO of a corporation, a corporation that does nothing but own his car for him. Buyers who pursue this option generally budget in an extra thousand dollars.

These were daunting problems, but the final hitch was more personal.

"Can you drive?" my friend Alejo once asked during a road trip to Guanacaste.

"Of course," I said.

"Can you drive stick?" he said.

"Just automatic."

"Ah," he scoffed. "So you *can't* really drive."

Costa Rica's topography is rough-and-tumble, and although the economy is the second-best in Central America, the roads are generally considered the worst. Most cars on sale are manual, and most student drivers learn with a clutch. Even if we found the ideal car, I might require days or weeks to learn how to drive it.

Buying a car was among our proudest achievements, because we did it in the most Tico way possible. We didn't find the right classified ad or spot a "*Se Vende*" sign in a car window. We simply met the right person, and he introduced us to his father. This is how real business has been done since time immemorial, and it is the rule by which most Ticos live: If you can't do it yourself, find a relative who can.

Kylan had volunteered at the Children's Hospital since the month we arrived, and she had met a lot of people. One young physician, Mario, was doing his rounds at the hospital, and although he was disappointed to find out that Kylan was married, they became good friends. One day, Kylan mentioned our search for a car and how much time and energy we had burned.

"Oh," said Mario, who brightened. "Well, my Papi sells cars. You should meet him."

"He *sells* cars? Like he has a dealership?"

"Actually, he flies to the United States, finds cars, drives them to Florida, and then has them shipped to Costa Rica."

Indeed, used cars are *so* expensive that Mario's father's business was actually more lucrative than selling cars already in Costa Rica. The most expensive part, said Mario, was paying the *impuesto*—import tax—when the vehicle arrived in Puerto Limón. In fact, Mario's father had a Nissan Sentra at that very moment. The car was cheap, reliable, easy to fix, and *automatic*.

Kylan had set her heart on a more muscular vehicle, a Jeep or SUV that could roll over rubble or barge its way through flash-floods, but I had suggested otherwise.

"Most of the places we're going are on regular highways," I said. "And frankly, if we're headed to a place like Monteverde, I'd rather let an expert drive us."

Old-fashioned as Costa Rica can be, the country is astoundingly automotive. While ranchers still mount horses and farmhands ride bicycles to work, the vast majority of Costa Ricans rely on engines to get around. Buses are always packed, and they stop in the remotest villages. Winding mountain roads have transformed into well-trafficked highways. My friend Andres said that to reach Jacó, the nearest beach town to San José, his family used to drive six hours; now it takes less than two on the four-lane *pista*. The roads aren't always smooth, but a regular sedan could take us far and wide.

So Kylan relented. We would try for the Nissan.

Of all our hurdles in Costa Rica, buying a car was by far the most pleasurable. Mario introduced us to his father, Paco. Paco's wife brought us iced tea. We sat on their living room couch and talked about the car. Paco invited us into the garage and we inspected it. Kylan hopped into the driver's seat and drove around the neighborhood. We said yes. We returned a few days later, after Paco had personally installed a radio and spare tire and washed the car down. He drove us to his attorney, a chirpy woman in Desamparados, who prepared all the papers in her cluttered home office. Then Paco drove us to various offices to have the car registered and inspected. By the time we were done, we wanted to adopt Paco as our surrogate grandfather.

Paco was sparkle-eyed and gentle as a saint. For every requisite wait, Paco had another question for us—where we got married, why we lived in Costa Rica, what we did for a living—and time eased past. The car itself seemed as solid as a 1998 Nissan could be: The white surface gleamed, the interior smelled fresh, the cushions had been vacuumed of every spec of dust. The engine vibrated a little, but it ran nicely. For $5,000, we couldn't possibly hope for better.

When we returned to Paco's house, Mario was standing outside. Everyone hugged and kissed cheeks and exchanged the usual well wishes: "*Hasta luego*" and "*Vaya con Dios*" and a dozen other exhortations. Finally we slipped into the car. Kylan revved the engine, we waved at Mario's family through the windshield, and we headed down the street, frantic with excitement.

Two days later, Kylan sheepishly asked me, "Is it wrong that I *love* driving in San José?"

"No," I said. "I know *exactly* what you're talking about."

We had long feared Central Valley traffic. The chaotic one-way streets and devil-may-care drivers struck us as a perfect vehicular storm, and every block was saturated in danger: Cars switched lanes on a whim, motorcycles weaved everywhere, unattended children strayed into the shoulder, and vendors stood in the middle of highways and waved bags of cashews. The potholes were cavernous. Speed bumps were often left unpainted, and we had to brake at the last second to save our axle. We had no idea why some intersections bore both stop signs *and* blinking traffic lights. Buses and motorcycles weaved perilously around each other, as if they alone enjoyed right-of-way.

Yet for those first few days, the experience of dodging pedestrians and guessing which lanes would abruptly end thrilled us, and we found every excuse to run an errand and therefore drive somewhere.

The first weekend, we decided to drive to Jacó. At long last, this was a trip we could take on a Saturday morning without hours of planning. No taxi to the bus station. No overcrowded *autobús*. No consulting a jumble of online itineraries. No more feeling like a tourist. We could just *go*.

On the way to Jacó, the highway crosses the Tárcoles River, a chocolate-colored waterway that bends lazily through its valley. The highway bridge is long and low, and beneath its concrete pylons lies a bask of enormous crocodiles. The man-eating reptiles are famous and attract visitors from around the world. Shops cluster together just before the bridge, and there's always a *guachimán* ushering cars into the gravel lot.

On a bus, you can't stop. You simply watch the *sodas* and souvenir shops drift past. On a hot day, I might not even notice, because I would be asleep, my skull pressed against the bus window.

But in the car, we could stop. We could chat briefly with the *guachimán* about the weather in conversational Spanish. We could enter the *soda* and ask for a *pipa*, and we could drink its water through a straw. We could browse the tapestries hanging from a clothesline and pick our favorite, then buy it on the spot, because we had been seeking a wall hanging for our bedroom for ages. We could stroll down the bridge's walkway as trucks flew past, then look down at the crocodiles sunning themselves below. We could shake our heads and smile in disbelief, because this wasn't some luxury safari but our actual lives. We could whip out our phones and call scores of people and make dinner plans for that very night. We could finish our coconut and chop it in half and scoop our the rubbery white meat with a spoon—a skill we had never known before—and then discard the biodegradable shell. We could hop back in the car, toss the *guachimán* a 500-*colón* coin, and reverse into the road. We could fly over the bridge, rise into the hills, take curves, drop toward the sea. For the first time in nearly a year, we felt like we could do damn near anything.

Acknowledgments

Pretty much everyone wants to move to paradise to write a book, and very few have the chance to do so. I am implausibly lucky, and on so many levels: It was David Boddiger, editor of *The Tico Times*, who decided to hire me, even though I spoke no Spanish and knew almost nothing about Costa Rica. It was a big risk, and I am forever grateful for that decision. Dave mentored me from the beginning, and he continues to do so every day—even on rough days when he has more important things to think about.

I am further indebted to my *compañeros* at the paper, a dysfunctional family of writers and photographers who have helped make life in Costa Rica so wonderful: Alberto "Beto" Font, Lindsay Fendt, Zach Dyer, Jill Replogle, Andres Madrigal, Laianer Arias, Karl Kahler, Fabiola Pomadera, Corey Kane, and Matt Levin. Most of these stories were assigned, green-lit, cultivated, and copyedited by Katherine Stanley Obando, Ashley Harrell, and Shelby Vittek. Under their care, I have enjoyed enormous editorial freedom and repeated excuses to hang out in weird places. Meanwhile, the paper's administration has navigated me through mounds of paperwork, and I will be forever grateful to Martha Gamboa, Cindy Vargas, and Mariana Loaiza for being so patient with their favorite *pelirrojo*.

This magnificent cover was the work of Haime Luna and Nathan Kukulski, who spent countless hours designing and putting it together, and Gabriela Wattson did a lovely job with the interior. Facing a labyrinth of confusing steps, it was Alonso Muñoz who helped navigate us through the Costa Rican publishing process.

Publishing this book was the perfect excuse to get to know Robin Kazmier, the master of all things books and birding. She took a malformed skeleton and gave it life, and I hope *The Green Season* is the first of many collaborations.

The Tico Times would not exist, nor would this book specifically, if not for the paper's owner, Jonathan Harris. Jonathan has poured his heart and soul into this paper, and he has encouraged me every day of *mi vida costarricense*. I have learned more about the Tico soul through our late-night discussions than in a dozen books and museums, although I'll admit that the tequila helped.

But the most gratitude goes to my wife, Kylan, who embarked on this insane Costa Rican journey with me. It's not every spouse who enthusiastically moves to Central America with you and then agrees to be a recurring character in your book. Thanks to Ky's perseverance and diehard attitude, our "green season" is more verdant than ever. I can't wait to see what happens next.